P9-AGU-485

OPPOSING
VIEWPOINTS®
SERIES

| Nuclear Weapons

Other Books of Related Interest

Opposing Viewpoints Series

America's Infrastructure and the Green Economy
Genocide
The U.S. Military

At Issue Series

Cyberwarfare
Guns: Conceal and Carry
Nuclear Anxiety

Current Controversies Series

America's Role in a Changing World
Cyberterrorism
Space: Tourism, Competition, Militarization

"Congress shall make no law … abridging the freedom of speech, or of the press."

First Amendment to the U.S. Constitution

The basic foundation of our democracy is the First Amendment guarantee of freedom of expression. The Opposing Viewpoints series is dedicated to the concept of this basic freedom and the idea that it is more important to practice it than to enshrine it.

OPPOSING
VIEWPOINTS®
SERIES

|Nuclear Weapons

Erica Grove, Book Editor

WITHDRAWN

GREENHAVEN
PUBLISHING

Published in 2023 by Greenhaven Publishing, LLC
2544 Clinton Street,
Buffalo NY 14224

Copyright © 2024 by Greenhaven Publishing, LLC

First Edition

All rights reserved. No part of this book may be reproduced in any form
without permission in writing from the publisher, except by a reviewer.

Articles in Greenhaven Publishing anthologies are often edited for length to meet page
requirements. In addition, original titles of these works are changed to clearly present
the main thesis and to explicitly indicate the author's opinion. Every effort is made to
ensure that Greenhaven Publishing accurately reflects the original intent of the authors.
Every effort has been made to trace the owners of the copyrighted material.

Cover image: Bordovski Yauheni/Shutterstock.com

Library of Congress CataloginginPublication Data

Names: Grove, Erica, editor.
Title: Nuclear weapons / edited by Erica Grove.
Description: First Edition. | New York : Greenhaven Publishing, 2024. | Series:
Opposing viewpoints | Includes bibliographic references and index.
Identifiers: ISBN 9781534509399 (pbk.) | ISBN 9781534509405 (library bound)
Subjects: LCSH: Nuclear nonproliferation--Juvenile literature.
Classification: LCC JZ5675.N883 2024 | DDC 327.1'747--dc23

Manufactured in the United States of America

Website: http://greenhavenpublishing.com

Contents

Chapter 1: Has the Nuclear Threat Reached a Crisis Point?

Chapter 2: Should the United States Possess Nuclear Weapons?

The Importance of Opposing Viewpoints

Perhaps every generation experiences a period in time in which the populace seems especially polarized, starkly divided on the important issues of the day and gravitating toward the far ends of the political spectrum and away from a consensus-facilitating middle ground. The world that today's students are growing up in and that they will soon enter into as active and engaged citizens is deeply fragmented in just this way. Issues relating to terrorism, immigration, women's rights, minority rights, race relations, health care, taxation, wealth and poverty, the environment, policing, military intervention, the proper role of government—in some ways, perennial issues that are freshly and uniquely urgent and vital with each new generation—are currently roiling the world.

If we are to foster a knowledgeable, responsible, active, and engaged citizenry among today's youth, we must provide them with the intellectual, interpretive, and critical-thinking tools and experience necessary to make sense of the world around them and of the all-important debates and arguments that inform it. After all, the outcome of these debates will in large measure determine the future course, prospects, and outcomes of the world and its peoples, particularly its youth. If they are to become successful members of society and productive and informed citizens, students need to learn how to evaluate the strengths and weaknesses of someone else's arguments, how to sift fact from opinion and fallacy, and how to test the relative merits and validity of their own opinions against the known facts and the best possible available information. The landmark series Opposing Viewpoints has been providing students with just such critical-thinking skills and exposure to the debates surrounding society's most urgent contemporary issues for many years, and it continues to serve this essential role with undiminished commitment, care, and rigor.

The key to the series's success in achieving its goal of sharpening students' critical-thinking and analytic skills resides in its title—

Opposing Viewpoints. In every intriguing, compelling, and engaging volume of this series, readers are presented with the widest possible spectrum of distinct viewpoints, expert opinions, and informed argumentation and commentary, supplied by some of today's leading academics, thinkers, analysts, politicians, policy makers, economists, activists, change agents, and advocates. Every opinion and argument anthologized here is presented objectively and accorded respect. There is no editorializing in any introductory text or in the arrangement and order of the pieces. No piece is included as a "straw man," an easy ideological target for cheap point-scoring. As wide and inclusive a range of viewpoints as possible is offered, with no privileging of one particular political ideology or cultural perspective over another. It is left to each individual reader to evaluate the relative merits of each argument— as he or she sees it, and with the use of ever-growing critical-thinking skills—and grapple with his or her own assumptions, beliefs, and perspectives to determine how convincing or successful any given argument is and how the reader's own stance on the issue may be modified or altered in response to it.

This process is facilitated and supported by volume, chapter, and selection introductions that provide readers with the essential context they need to begin engaging with the spotlighted issues, with the debates surrounding them, and with their own perhaps shifting or nascent opinions on them. In addition, guided reading and discussion questions encourage readers to determine the authors' point of view and purpose, interrogate and analyze the various arguments and their rhetoric and structure, evaluate the arguments' strengths and weaknesses, test their claims against available facts and evidence, judge the validity of the reasoning, and bring into clearer, sharper focus the reader's own beliefs and conclusions and how they may differ from or align with those in the collection or those of their classmates.

Research has shown that reading comprehension skills improve dramatically when students are provided with compelling, intriguing, and relevant "discussable" texts. The subject matter of these collections could not be more compelling, intriguing, or urgently relevant to today's students and the world they are poised to inherit. The anthologized articles and the reading and discussion questions that are included with them also provide the basis for stimulating, lively, and passionate classroom debates. Students who are compelled to anticipate objections to their own argument and identify the flaws in those of an opponent read more carefully, think more critically, and steep themselves in relevant context, facts, and information more thoroughly. In short, using discussable text of the kind provided by every single volume in the Opposing Viewpoints series encourages close reading, facilitates reading comprehension, fosters research, strengthens critical thinking, and greatly enlivens and energizes classroom discussion and participation. The entire learning process is deepened, extended, and strengthened.

For all of these reasons, Opposing Viewpoints continues to be exactly the right resource at exactly the right time—when we most need to provide readers with the critical-thinking tools and skills that will not only serve them well in school but also in their careers and their daily lives as decision-making family members, community members, and citizens. This series encourages respectful engagement with and analysis of opposing viewpoints and fosters a resulting increase in the strength and rigor of one's own opinions and stances. As such, it helps make readers "future ready," and that readiness will pay rich dividends for the readers themselves, for the citizenry, for our society, and for the world at large.

Introduction

"Nuclear weapons pervade our thinking. Control our behavior. Administer our societies. Inform our dreams. They bury themselves like meat hooks deep in the base of our brains."

- Arundhati Roy,
Indian author

From 1942 to 1945, the U.S., the United Kingdom, and Canada set to work developing the atomic bomb in a project known as the Manhattan Project. World War II was raging on, and the U.S. and its allies wanted to develop a weapon so destructive that it would force the Axis—Nazi Germany, Italy, and Japan—to surrender. Most of the work of designing nuclear weapons for the Manhattan Project was completed in Los Alamos, New Mexico, under the leadership of nuclear physicist Robert Oppenheimer.[1] In July 1945, the first atomic bomb was successfully detonated, and the world would never be the same.[2]

The first actual application of the nuclear weapons developed by the Manhattan Project occurred in August 1945, when the U.S. dropped atomic bombs on the Japanese cities of Hiroshima and Nagasaki. It is difficult to determine exactly how many people died as a result of these attacks, but estimates generally range between 110,000 and 210,000, most of whom were civilians.[3] The unprecedented scale of death and destruction caused by nuclear weapons brought about two divergent responses: some countries wanted to harness the power of nuclear weapons for themselves by developing and stockpiling more nuclear weapons, and some countries, individuals, and organizations wanted to completely eliminate nuclear weapons to ensure a tragedy of this magnitude would never happen again.

In the aftermath of World War II, the U.S. and the Soviet Union (USSR, now Russia)—formerly allies during the war—became rivals in a conflict known as the Cold War (1947–1991). This historical period marked a time of great tension between the two countries as both tried to exert the most influence over the post–World War II geopolitical landscape. One way the U.S. and USSR tried to exert their power was by developing large nuclear arsenals. At its peak in 1967, the U.S. possessed 31,255 nuclear weapons, and the USSR claimed a peak arsenal of approximately 45,000 nuclear warheads in 1986.[4,5] In the years since the Cold War, the size of the U.S. and Russia's nuclear stockpiles has shrunken considerably, but a nuclear rivalry persists between them.

This is made evident by Russian President Vladimir Putin's threats to use nuclear weapons in Russia's war against Ukraine in 2022, a threat that raised alarm among the U.S. and its allies. However, Russia is no longer the U.S.'s only nuclear threat. China, North Korea, Iran, and even terrorist organizations pose potential threats to U.S. national security through access to nuclear weapons.

Since the devastating capabilities of nuclear weapons were first unleashed in 1945, people have debated whether they should exist at all. Many people feel that it would be a tragedy for them to be used again in any context, and that the only way to prevent another nuclear event—either intentional or accidental—is to dismantle all nuclear weapons. This is known as nuclear disarmament, and it differs from nuclear nonproliferation in that the latter focuses on ensuring that no new nuclear weapons are created rather than eliminating nuclear weapons that already exist. The United Nations (UN) has played an instrumental role in negotiations around nuclear nonproliferation and disarmament. Its Treaty on the Non-Proliferation of Nuclear Weapons (NPT) was first introduced for signature in 1968 and entered into force in 1970, and 190 parties—including the U.S. and the USSR—signed.[6] Its objective was to stop the spread of nuclear weapons, and it is considered a landmark treaty. Individual countries have also made treaties among themselves to limit nuclear weapons, including a number of treaties between the U.S. and the USSR/Russia.

However, efforts to eliminate all nuclear weapons have faced significant challenges, as made evident by the UN's struggles to create a legally binding treaty prohibiting nuclear weapons, known as the Treaty on the Prohibition of Nuclear Weapons (TPNW). This treaty was opened for signature in 2017 and entered into force in 2021 after being adopted by 122 states, but no nuclear weapon states (such as the U.S. and Russia) signed the treaty.[7] Until nuclear weapon states agree to nuclear disarmament, it will not be possible to completely eliminate nuclear weapons.

With chapters titled "Has the Nuclear Threat Reached a Crisis Point?," "Should the United States Possess Nuclear Weapons?," "Is Nuclear Disarmament Possible?," and "Is There a Significant Chance of Nuclear War?," the viewpoints in *Opposing Viewpoints: Nuclear Weapons* consider the history, present, and future of nuclear weapons from a wide range of perspectives. They consider the role of nuclear weapons in international relations and explore the question of whether a world without nuclear weapons is possible.

Notes

1. History.com Editors, "Manhattan Project," *History.com*, April 19, 2022. https://www.history.com/topics/world-war-ii/the-manhattan-project.
2. *Ibid.*
3. Alex Wellerstein, "Counting the Dead at Hiroshima and Nagasaki," *Bulletin of the Atomic Scientists*, August 4, 2020. https://thebulletin.org/2020/08/counting-the-dead-at-hiroshima-and-nagasaki/.
4. "Nuclear Stockpile Transparency," National Nuclear Security Administration. https://www.energy.gov/nnsa/nuclear-stockpile-transparency.
5. Hans M. Kristensen and Robert S. Norris, "Global Nuclear Stockpiles, 1945–2006," *Bulletin of the Atomic Scientists*, July/August 2006. https://journals.sagepub.com/doi/pdf/10.2968/062004017.
6. "Treaty on the Non-Proliferation of Nuclear Weapons," United Nations Office on Disarmament Affairs. https://treaties.unoda.org/t/npt.
7. "Treaty on the Prohibition of Nuclear Weapons," United Nations Office on Disarmament Affairs. https://www.un.org/disarmament/wmd/nuclear/tpnw/.

CHAPTER 1

Has the Nuclear Threat Reached a Crisis Point?

Chapter Preface

Since the invention of the atomic bomb, the only instance in which it has been used in warfare was during World War II, when the United States dropped atomic bombs on the cities of Hiroshima and Nagasaki in Japan in August 1945. The devastating destructive capabilities of these weapons became immediately evident. Because of the immense scale of death and destruction wreaked by the atomic bomb, countries understandably have been reluctant to use them again. In large part this is attributed to mutually assured destruction, meaning that if one country decides to attack another country with a nuclear weapon, it is safe to assume that the attacked country or one of its allies will attack the aggressor with a nuclear weapon in retaliation.

However, as a result of the doctrine of mutually assured destruction, various countries have stockpiled nuclear weapons in order to ensure other countries are aware of their nuclear capabilities. This has been particularly true of the United States and Russia, which possess approximately 90 percent of the world's nuclear weapons arsenal.[1] As of 2022, nine countries were estimated to have approximately 12,700 nuclear warheads.[2]

The U.S. and its allies face nuclear threats from rogue states, or countries that are aggressive and seek to upset the balance of power by disregarding international treaties and diplomatic efforts. The rogue states that possess or are suspected of possessing or developing a nuclear arsenal include Russia, North Korea, and Iran. Russia in particular has become a source of concern in recent years, as Russian President Vladimir Putin put the country's nuclear weapons program on high alert and ordered the nuclear program "to a special mode of combat duty" in response to the invasion of Ukraine in February 2022.[3] In addition to the threat from other countries, concerns exist that terrorist groups could come into possession of nuclear weapons, adding another element of danger into the mix.

But despite the fact that a wide variety of nations and groups pose a nuclear threat, multiple authors of viewpoints in this chapter argue that the nuclear threat is lower than it was during the Cold War (1947–1991), when there were various moments of high nuclear tension. The viewpoints in this chapter consider the question of what comprises the nuclear threat today and how it compares to the threat faced at various points in the history of nuclear weapons.

Notes

1. "Global Nuclear Arsenals Grow as States Continue to Modernize–New SIPRI Yearbook Out Now," Stockholm International Peace Research Institute (SIPRI), June 14, 2021. https://www.sipri.org/media/press-release/2021/global-nuclear-arsenals-grow-states-continue-modernize-new-sipri-yearbook-out-now.
2. "Status of World Nuclear Forces," Federation of American Scientists (FAS). https://fas.org/issues/nuclear-weapons/status-world-nuclear-forces/.
3. David M. Herszenhorn, "Putin Puts Russian Nuclear Forces on High Alert," *Politico*, February 27, 2022.

> *"In short, the risk of nuclear weapons use is not higher now than at any time since World War Two."*

Nuclear Tension Is Not as High Today as It Was During the Cold War

Sam Dudin

In this viewpoint, Sam Dudin argues that the statement then-Director of the UN Institute for Disarmament Research Renata Dwan gave in May 2019 regarding an increased risk of nuclear weapon use was misleading and inaccurate. Dudin asserts that there have been numerous instances since World War II when the nuclear threat was considerably higher than it is in the present. Most of these instances were during the Cold War (1947–1991), particularly during the Cuban Missile Crisis (October 1962), when both the U.S. and the Soviet Union were prepared to use nuclear force. At the time this viewpoint was originally published, Sam Dudin was a UK nuclear policy research fellow at the Royal United Services Institute.

As you read, consider the following questions:

1. What reasons does Renata Dwan give for the higher risk of nuclear weapon use, according to this viewpoint?
2. What historical conflicts does Dudin argue caused the nuclear risk to be higher than it is today?

"Risk of Nuclear Weapons Use Still Lower Than During Cold War", was first published on May 28, 2019, and was written by Sam Dudin, then UK Nuclear Policy Research Fellow at the Royal United Services Institute. Reprinted by permission.

3. What does Dudin say were the negative effects of Dwan's statement on the nuclear threat?

Renata Dwan, director of the UN Institute for Disarmament Research (UNIDIR), told reporters in Geneva on 21 May that the risk of nuclear weapons being used is at its highest since World War II. This is not "use" in the sense of "the nuclear deterrent is in use every day of every week all around the year", as argued by MP Julian Lewis in a recent House of Commons debate; this is "use" in the sense of nuclear warfare.

Dwan mentioned various reasons for this increased risk, including nuclear modernisation programmes, the erosion of traditional arms control, new types of war, the prevalence of armed groups and private sector forces, new technologies and the blurring of the line between offence and defence.

Regarding the Treaty on the Prohibition of Nuclear Weapons, Dwan stated:

> I think that it's genuinely a call to recognize—and this has been somewhat missing in the media coverage of the issues—that the risks of nuclear war are particularly high now, and the risks of the use of nuclear weapons, for some of the factors I pointed out, are higher now than at any time since World War II.

The main problem with Dwan's position is that, although the risk of nuclear weapons use has increased in recent years, the risk was higher at several points during the Cold War, including during the Berlin Crisis (1958–1961), the Cuban Missile Crisis (1962), the Sino–Soviet border conflict (1969), the Yom Kippur War (1973) and exercise Able Archer 83 (1983).

Two incidents during the Cuban Missile Crisis were particularly risky, and both involved tactical, counterforce nuclear weapons. As noted in Bagwell and Dudin's 2013 Discretion Analysis Final Report, during the crisis a U-2 spy plane undertook an air sampling mission, testing the atmosphere over the Arctic Ocean for residue from Soviet nuclear tests. Since the flight plan did not take the aircraft closer than 100 miles to Soviet airspace, it was not considered risky and continued as scheduled despite the ongoing crisis. Unfortunately, the U-2 accidentally crossed several hundred miles into Soviet airspace, apparently due to a navigational error. Soviet fighters scrambled to intercept and American fighters rushed to protect the U-2. Since US forces were at DEFCON 3, the American fighters carried nuclear air-to-air missiles rather than their usual conventional weapons. While in theory the nuclear missiles could only be used on the authority of the president, there were no physical means to prevent a pilot firing the missiles at his own discretion. Fortunately, the U-2 reached U.S. airspace and landed safely without being intercepted.

The second incident occurred on 27 October 1962, the day before the crisis ended, and just hours after a U-2 spy plane had been shot down over Cuba. Early in October, the 69th torpedo submarine brigade of the Soviet Navy had been ordered "to strengthen the defense of the island of Cuba". The brigade consisted of four diesel-electric Foxtrot-class submarines, each armed with 22 torpedoes with a range of 19 km. Unknown to the U.S., one torpedo on each submarine had a 10-kilotonne nuclear warhead.

The U.S. issued a message stating that practice depth charges would be used to force blockade-running Soviet submarines to surface. However, one of the submarines, B-59, had for two days been unable to come to periscope depth to use its antenna. As such, it had not received that message. When U.S. naval vessels followed through on the threat of using low-yield depth charges to bring B-59 to the surface, the submarine's senior officers argued about whether or not to respond with their nuclear torpedo. The submarine's commander, Captain Valentin Grigorievitch, ordered the officer who was assigned to the nuclear torpedo to assemble it to battle readiness, adding:

> Maybe the war has already started up there, while we are doing summersaults here… We're gonna blast them now! We will die, but we will sink them all—we will not become the shame of the fleet.

His second-in-command, Vasili Arkhipov, persuaded Grigorievitch not to fire, but to surface and wait for orders from Moscow.

"The lesson from this", argued director of the National Security Archive, Thomas Blanton, "is that a guy called Vasili Arkhipov saved the world." Historian Arthur M. Schlesinger Jr. observed, "This was not only the most dangerous moment of the Cold War. It was the most dangerous moment in human history."

While the Cuban Missile Crisis is arguably the most well-known nuclear crisis, the Sino–Soviet border conflict of 1969 is probably the least. On 2 March 1969, Chinese soldiers killed a group of Soviet border guards on Zhenbao Island, a disputed island in the Ussuri River. In the following months, several battles were fought along the Russian–Chinese border. Nuclear threats were part of the Soviet strategy to resolve this conflict, but China did not think the threats were credible: that is, until 27 August when CIA Director Richard Helms told the press that the Soviet Union had approached foreign governments to gauge their reactions to a potential Soviet pre-emptive nuclear strike on China. By mid-October, China's fear of a Soviet nuclear attack was such that the central leadership, including Mao Zedong, fled Beijing. China's fledgling nuclear forces were ordered to full alert on 18 October, the only time this has occurred. Two days later, negotiations with Russia began, ending the conflict.

Despite increasing nuclear risks in recent years, there have been no reports of national leaders fleeing their country's capital city out of fear of a nuclear strike. Fighters with air-to-air nuclear missiles are not being scrambled to protect aircraft from enemy interceptors. And it is unlikely that there are any naval captains in recent years who have shouted "We're gonna blast them now! We will die, but we will sink them all" while ordering a nuclear torpedo to be readied for firing.

In short, the risk of nuclear weapons use is not higher now than at any time since World War II. However, Renata Dwan's statement on nuclear risk was published by various news outlets around the world, which accurately assessed that such a statement was newsworthy. Unfortunately, this has potentially misinformed and scared millions of people around the world.

> *"This 'nuclear learning' during the Cold War will require a reboot for adaptation to the so-called 'third nuclear age' of the early-to-mid 21st century."*

Nuclear Arms Control Is More Difficult than Ever Before

Stephen J. Cimbala and Lawrence J. Korb

In this viewpoint, Stephen J. Cimbala and Lawrence J. Korb assert that the contemporary political situation and technological situation have made nuclear arms control increasingly difficult. Weapons are now able to be launched much faster than they were in the past, and space is now a new arena for nuclear defense and potentially attacks. Cyberattacks and information warfare also threaten military operations. New strategies for promoting nuclear deterrence and arms control must be found that take into account the current status of nuclear defense. Stephen J. Cimbala is a distinguished professor of political science at Pennsylvania State University, Brandywine. Lawrence J. Korb is a senior fellow at the Center for American Progress and an adjunct professor of security studies at Georgetown University.

As you read, consider the following questions:

1. According to this viewpoint, who are the three major nuclear players today?

"Nuclear arms control: Still necessary, but more difficult than ever," by Stephen J. Cimbala and Lawrence J. Korb, Bulletin of the Atomic Scientists, April 5, 2022. Reprinted by permission.

2. Why is space important to the United States' arms control defensive strategy?

3. According to the authors, why are countries reluctant to reduce or eliminate their nuclear arsenals?

Russia's war against Ukraine has worsened an already deteriorating political relationship with the United States and NATO. The fraught atmosphere between Washington and Moscow also threatened to affect the issue of nuclear arms control. The New Strategic Arms Reduction Treaty (New START), which Russia and the United States extended for five years in 2021, is the last remaining nuclear arms control agreement between the two powers. If New START is thrown overboard or dies of inattention, there would be no remaining treaty to constrain the advent of a second nuclear arms race, one potentially more dangerous than U.S.–Soviet competition during the Cold War.[1]

Some question whether arms control is even possible in the new world order that was already taking shape before Russia's invasion of Ukraine. Challenges to nuclear arms control come from shifts in global political alignments, new technologies, and domestic pressures for nuclear modernization.[2] During the Cold War, the arms race was largely dominated by American and Soviet superpowers. Eventually, it became clear to both sides that there was no "last move" in strategy, or any technology breakthrough, that would provide nuclear superiority relative to the opponent. Mutual deterrence based on assured retaliation was accepted as a matter of fact. And although the Cold War witnessed some close calls in terms of crisis management, both the Americans and the Soviets learned that competition in nuclear risk-taking had to operate under tacit and explicit rules of the road to avoid an outbreak of nuclear war based on misperceptions of enemy intent, technology failures, or miscalculated escalation.

This "nuclear learning" during the Cold War will require a reboot for adaptation to the so-called "third nuclear age" of the early-to-mid 21st century. In terms of nuclear weapons deployed on intercontinental launchers, there are now three major players. China's rise as an aspiring peer competitor with the United States and Russia changes the game of deterrence and defense against nuclear attack.[3] Although China currently deploys only several hundred warheads on long-range launchers, this number is likely to grow rapidly as the People's Republic fleshes out its triad of land-based missiles, bombers, and submarine-launched ballistic missiles.[4]

Technology has also complicated the challenge of maintaining nuclear deterrence stability, in several ways. First, hypersonic weapons can travel within the atmosphere at supersonic speeds and (potentially) evade antimissile defenses. Their speed reduces

ARMS CONTROL AGREEMENTS BETWEEN THE U.S. AND RUSSIA

Four years after the United States first tested and used nuclear weapons, the Soviet Union ushered in a new nuclear era with its first nuclear test on August 29, 1949. Within a few years, the arms race was in full steam as the Soviets grew their arsenal and conducted 715 atmospheric and underground nuclear tests from 1949-1990. At its peak in 1986, the Soviet Union had around 40,000 nuclear warheads in its stockpile.

Through a number of bilateral arms control agreements with the United States at the end of and after the Cold War, the Russian arsenal was reduced significantly. Today, Russia maintains a stockpile of an estimated 6,372 nuclear warheads, 1,572 of which are deployed on strategic land-based ballistic missiles, submarine-launched ballistic missiles, and heavy bombers. Approximately 870 more strategic warheads and 1,870 non-strategic warheads are in reserve with an additional estimated 2,060 warheads awaiting dismantlement.

Russia and the United States together still hold more than 90% of the world's nuclear arsenal, however, so it is imperative to maintain civil relations between the two countries to reduce the number of nuclear weapons and eliminate the risk of nuclear war. For decades, the time between detection of enemy missile launch and the arrival of enemy weapons at their targets.[5] Hypersonic weapons increase first-strike vulnerability for some components of the U.S. strategic retaliatory forces: silo-based intercontinental ballistic missiles (ICBMs) and unalerted bombers. Leaders may feel more pressure to launch potentially vulnerable missile forces "on warning" rather than lose them.

Second, there is the growing interest in missile defenses. Although no missile-defense systems will invalidate the effectiveness of large-scale nuclear attacks over the near term, promising technologies may create partially effective systems for national defense and more preclusive systems for theater or local protection against missile strikes.[6] These new technologies

U.S. presidents and Members of Congress from both parties have supported verifiable arms control treaties beginning with the Nuclear Test Ban Treaty through the START treaties. With the end of the Soviet Union, significant focus was placed on reducing fissile materials in Russia through the Nunn-Lugar Cooperate Threat Reduction (CTR) program and eliminating nuclear weapons from the former Soviet states of Ukraine, Belarus, and Kazakhstan.

Today, with U.S.-Russian relations at a post-Cold War low, and as both countries modernize their nuclear arsenals, the reality of a new nuclear arms race underscores the need for sensible non-proliferation and arms control cooperation. Despite this, the Trump administration withdrew from a number of critical arms control agreements, including the Intermediate-Range Nuclear Forces (INF) Treaty and the Open Skies Treaty. In early 2021, the Biden administration reached an agreement with Russia to extend the New START treaty until February 2026, the only remaining arms control treaty between the world's two largest arsenals. With this extension in place, the United States and Russia should begin talks to expand on further mutual reductions and other areas of concern, including non-strategic nuclear weapons, missile defenses, and other emerging technologies.

"U.S.-Russian Strategic Arms Control Agreements," Center for Arms Control and Non-Proliferation.

include drone swarms, ground- or space-based lasers or beams, unmanned aerial vehicles with air-to-ground strike weapons, and cyber "left of launch" techniques for aborting or distorting enemy launch and control systems.

Third, space has emerged as a medium for competitive strategy and possible conflict. Creation of the U.S. Space Force recognized space as a conflict domain along with land, sea, air, and cyber. [7] The United States depends upon space for reconnaissance, navigation, targeting, early warning of missile attack, and other missions. Destruction or interference with American space assets could delay or forestall military operations otherwise global in reach and timely in effect.[8] In addition, space-based missile defenses will have to be protected from "defense suppression" of their satellites and-or ground links.

Deterring attacks against space-based defenses may require deployment of specially tasked defensive satellites maintaining keep-out zones around the defenses. The problem is not hypothetical. Existing U.S. satellites in various orbits are already being tracked in real time by Russian and Chinese satellites in rendezvous-and-proximity operations.[9] Technically, such operations may be as innocent as satellite repairs, but the same technology would enable rendezvous-and-proximity satellites to disable or destroy unfriendly satellites.[10] In sum, the relationship between space-based defenses and deterrence is at least three sided: space-based components of a ballistic missile defense architecture must be survivable; defense suppression attacks against space-based missile defense must be deterred by denial (deterrence by punishment after the fact is too late); and deterrence of attacks in space requires resilient command, control, and communications that degrade gracefully, if at all, in the face of enemy initiatives.

A fourth aspect of the 21st century new world order is information and cyberwar. Today, cyber is the enabler for conflict in all other domains.[11] Digitally empowered U.S. forces maintain superiority across land, sea, air, and space domains. It follows that cyber defense and offense must keep up with pacing threats.

[12] But there's a problem: The United States has more apparent success in offensive than defensive cyberwar, partly because our democratic political system and dynamic market-based economy cannot be protected only by government efforts. The private sector must cooperate with the U.S. government to quickly detect threats to cybersecurity and to apply appropriate denial of access or defeat of malware intrusions.

Today, Russia and China view cyberwar as a cost-effective way to steal American technology and intellectual property. Russian war planning includes options for the use of strategic cyber operations against military and other targets. The use of information warfare and cyberattacks is also prominent in China's emphasis on "unrestricted warfare." Cyber operations come in two varieties: attacks on computers, networks, and their supporting infrastructure and information operations, more specific to the war of ideas and images. In its war against Ukraine in 2022, for example, Russian information operations have fallen far short of their mark. Russian disinformation and deception operations were clumsy, transparent, and ultimately ineffective. They lost the information war within a week of fighting.

A fifth challenge for nuclear arms control in a 21st-century context lies in the control of nuclear proliferation. How do we convince any existing nuclear weapons state to give up its nuclear arsenal if experience teaches that nukes are the guarantor against imposed regime change? It would not be unreasonable for some states feeling threatened by nuclear-armed or nuclear-aspiring neighbors to consider developing their own arsenals.

Succeeding in the 21st-century nuclear arms control era must begin with a willingness on the part of the leaders in Russia, the United States, and China—and later, other nuclear weapons states—to establish working groups of experts to explore the new world of nuclear deterrence and arms control. The desired outcome would be a series of policy papers addressing issues such as:

- How do different countries understand the concept of arms control, given new technology and rising state actors?

- How much is enough, in the way of nuclear weapons and delivery systems, for each state to meet its basic security needs?
- How will the evolution of space and cyber as conflict domains influence each state's definition of its minimum-security requirements?
- What is each state's view of the relationship between offensive strike weapons and missile and aircraft defenses, relative to nuclear strategic stability and deterrence?
- And how will advanced technologies for conventional warfare change ideas about conventional and nuclear deterrence?

The challenges facing future nuclear arms control are daunting—but not impossible—to meet.

Notes

[1] For background, see: Lawrence J. Korb, "Why it could (but shouldn't) be the end of the arms control era," *Bulletin of the Atomic Scientists*, October 23, 2018, https://the bulletin.org/2018/10/why-it-could-but-shouldnt-be-the-end-of-the-arms-control-era.html. See also: Stephen J. Cimbala, *The United States, Russia and Nuclear Peace* (New York: Palgrave-Macmillan/Springer, 2020).

[2] For example, see: Patrick Tucker, "Why New Technology Is Making Nuclear Arms Control Harder," *Defense One*, March 14, 2022, https://www.defenseone. com/policy/2022/03/why-new-technology-making-nuclear-arms-control-harder/363135/. See also: Steven Pifer, "With US-Russian arms control treaties on shaky ground, the future is worrying," *Brookings*, April 25, 2019, in *Johnson's Russia List*2019 – #72 – April 29, 2019, davidjohnson@starpower.net

[3] William J. Broad and David E. Sanger, "A 2nd New Nuclear Missile Base for China, and Many Questions About Strategy," *New York Times*, July 6, 2021, https://www. nytimes.com/2021/07/26/us/politics/china-nuclear-weapons.html

[4] James M. Smith and Paul J. Bolt, eds. *China's Strategic Arsenal: Worldview, Doctrine, and Systems.* Washington, D.C.: Georgetown University Press, 2021. See also: Defense Intelligence Agency. *China: Military Power – Modernizing a Force to Fight and Win.* Washington, D.C. U.S. Defense Intelligence Agency, 2019, www.dia.mil.

[5] Ian Williams, *Adapting to the Hypersonic Era* (Washington, D.C. Center for Strategic and International Studies, (November 2020), 3, https://defense360.csis.org/adapting-to-the-hypersonic-era/

[6] Michaela Dodge, "Missile Defense Reckoning Is Coming: Will the United States Choose to be Vulnerable to All Long-Range Missiles?" Fairfax, Va.: National Institute for Public Policy, August 20, 2020, <www.nipp.org>

Missile Defense Project, "Ground-based Midcourse Defense (GMD) System," (Washington, D.C.: Center for Strategic and International Studies, 2021, https:// missilethreat.csis.org/system/gmd/. Skepticism is expressed in: John Mecklin "Why *Star Wars* should remain a cinematic fantasy," *Bulletin of the Atomic Scientists*, no. 4 (2019, pp. 135-136, https://thebulletin.org/2019/06/why-should-remain-a-cinematic-fantasy/

[7] U.S. Department of Defense, *U.S. Space Defense Strategy, Summary*. Washington, D.C. U.S. Department of Defense, June 2020. https://media.defense.gov/2020/Jun/17/2002317391/-1/-1/1/2020_DEFENSE_SPACE_STRATEGY_SUMMARY. PDF

[8] James Clay Moltz, "The Changing Dynamics of Twenty-First-Century Space Power," *Strategic Studies Quarterly*, no. 1 (Spring 2019), pp. 66-94.

[9] Marissa Martin, Kaila Pfrang and Brian Weeden. *Chinese Military and Intelligence Rendezvous and Proximity Operations*. Secure World Foundation, April 2021, <www.swfound.org>

[10] Lawrence J. Korb, "The focus of US military efforts in outer space should be… arms control," *Bulletin of the Atomic Scientists*, no. 4 (2019), pp. 148-150, *DOI: 10.1080/00963402.2019.1628471*

[11] See: P.W. Singer and Allan Friedman, *Cybersecurity and Cyberwar: What Everyone Needs to Know*. Oxford: Oxford University Press, 2014, and Martin C. Libicki. *Cyberdeterrence and Cyberwar*. Santa Monica, Calif.: RAND Corporation, 2009.

[12] Catherine A.Theohary, "Defense Primer: Cyberspace Operations," Washington, D.C. Congressional Research Service, December 18, 2018, https://crsreports.congress. gov

> "Nuclear weapons fundamentally alter the relations between countries because each country is forced to think more pointedly about its adversaries' security imperatives."

Multiple Countries Still Possess Nuclear Weapons, but Numerous Other Countries Have Abandoned Nuclear Proliferation

George Friedman, Xander Snyder, and Cheyenne Ligon

In this viewpoint, George Friedman, Xander Snyder, and Cheyenne Ligon examine which countries currently are considered nuclear powers, which countries used to possess nuclear weapons but have since denuclearized, and which are in a state of nuclear latency. The U.S. and Russia both still possess thousands of nuclear warheads, but their current nuclear inventories are much smaller than their peak inventories during the Cold War. Although nuclear weapons still pose a significant threat, there are fewer nuclear weapons today than during the Cold War. George Friedman is the founder and chairman of Geopolitical Futures. Xander Snyder previously was an analyst with Geopolitical Futures and is now a real estate economist with First American. Cheyenne Ligon was a junior intelligence analyst with Geopolitical Futures and is currently a news reporter at CoinDesk.

"The Geopolitics of Nuclear Weapons - Geopolitical Futures," by George Friedman, Xander Snyder, and Cheyenne Ligon, Mauldin Economics, April 17, 2017. Reprinted by permission.

As you read, consider the following questions:

1. At the time this viewpoint was published in 2017, how many nuclear warheads did the U.S. have? How many did Russia have?
2. What are the three factors the authors list for why some countries have forfeited their nuclear arsenals?
3. How is nuclear latency defined in this viewpoint?

Nuclear bombs have a strange quality: They are a type of weapon that countries spend enormous sums of money to develop but don't actually intend to use. While chemical weapons have been frequently used in war, no country has detonated a nuclear bomb since the end of World War II.

Nuclear weapons are in their own category. Their efficacy comes from their ability to deter aggression, as the potential for massive devastation forces countries to rethink moves that threaten an adversary's essential national security interests. States, therefore, are unlikely to use nuclear weapons against one another. However, the risk of a nuclear attack would increase if they were to fall into the hands of non-state actors that follow a different set of calculations that don't necessarily take into account the defense of a predefined territory.

Nine countries currently have nuclear weapons with an assortment of delivery systems.

Current Nuclear Powers

World Nuclear Capabilities

COUNTRY	DEPLOYED	RESERVED
U.S.	1,740	2,740
Russia	1,800	2,700
France	300	0
China	0	270

U.K.	120	95
Pakistan	0	140
India	0	120
Israel	0	80
North Korea	0	~20

Sources: Federation of American Scientists' Nuclear Notebook; Institute for Science and International Security

There are three aspects of the global nuclear arsenal to keep in mind. The first is a distinction between deployed and reserve weapons. Deployed nuclear weapons are already attached to a delivery system and ready to use. Warheads in reserve still require this final attachment step before they can be delivered.

The second aspect is the three delivery systems that comprise the nuclear "triad": land-based missiles (usually ballistic missiles but sometimes also cruise missiles), submarine-launched missiles (SLBMs), and weapons carried by aircraft (usually bombers but sometimes air-to-surface cruise missiles loaded on fighters or fighter-bombers). Land-based ballistic missiles—especially intercontinental ballistic missiles (ICBM)—provide long-range strike capability within a short period. SLBMs have retaliation capabilities in the event that a country's land-based ballistic missile arsenal is destroyed in a first strike. Warheads on aircraft are more flexible, since bombers can be recalled after a strike has been ordered, but they are slower to reach their target than missiles (except in the case where bombers are already in flight and their target is nearby). Each nuclear country has a different mix of delivery capabilities, but only the United States and Russia are known to definitively possess a full triad, while China and India are suspected to have it.

The third aspect is the large portion of global nuclear arms held by the United States and Russia. Currently, the U.S. has approximately 4,480 warheads, and Russia has 4,500. These figures include both strategic warheads (which are meant to strike sites located far from any hypothetical battlefield) and nonstrategic, or tactical, warheads (which are intended to be used near a battlefield, and as a result, are usually less powerful). The size of these arsenals, however, pales in comparison to each country's peak inventory during the Cold War: The U.S. had 31,255 in 1967, and the Soviet Union had 40,159 in 1986.

Throughout the Cold War, the doctrine of mutually assured destruction required a sufficiently large force that would allow for a massive retaliation even if a first strike eliminated a large portion of a country's nuclear arsenal. Additionally, during most of the Cold War, delivery systems were not particularly accurate, which required that nuclear weapons have very large yields to reliably strike a target that might be located miles away from the point of detonation (many hydrogen bombs were in the several megaton range). As the accuracy of delivery systems improved, fewer nuclear warheads were required to maintain a credible deterrence threat, leading to a decline in both countries' arsenals.

Nuclear weapons fundamentally alter the relations between countries because each country is forced to think more pointedly about its adversaries' security imperatives. Developing a strong understanding of those imperatives is critical to avoiding a nuclear retaliation. While several "hot" wars and other tense moments occurred during the Cold War, none escalated to a direct confrontation between the Soviet Union and the U.S.

For a more recent example, consider the case of North Korea, which has received a lot of attention in the last week due to a recent missile test and the expectation of another nuclear test. It is a poor country whose nuclear program has allowed it to punch above its weight internationally and force superpowers to approach it with great caution. North Korea's deterrent capability would be eliminated the moment it uses a nuclear weapon, which would be akin to committing certain suicide. While many fear the irrationality of North Korea's leadership, Geopolitical Futures' current understanding of the regime is that it has persisted for decades throughout the Cold War and after the fall of the Soviet

Union because it is able to make cautious calculations and has continued to choose not to inflict destruction on itself.

Former Nuclear States

Several countries had nuclear weapons or weapons programs that were subsequently abandoned. Three factors contributed to these forfeitures: changes in geopolitical circumstances that decreased the need for nuclear deterrence, pressure from a major power that provided a guarantee under its own nuclear umbrella, and outside intervention that resulted in destruction of the weapons programs.

Belarus, Kazakhstan, and Ukraine all inherited nuclear weapons when the Soviet Union collapsed in 1991. Belarus was left in possession of 81 warheads and an assortment of nonstrategic nuclear weapons. Kazakhstan had 1,410 nuclear-tipped missiles. Ukraine was left with 1,900 strategic warheads and between 2,650 and 4,200 nonstrategic nuclear weapons, making it the third-largest nuclear arsenal in the world. All three countries signed the Nuclear Non-Proliferation Treaty (NPT) and returned the weapons to Russia by the mid-1990s to be dismantled.

South Africa is the only country that independently developed its nuclear weapons and subsequently forfeited them. The pro-apartheid government pursued nuclear energy and weapons development from the 1960s to the '80s, eventually producing six nuclear weapons. In 1989, the program was stopped as apartheid came to an end and the government of F.W. de Klerk handed power over to the African National Congress. The weapons and associated facilities were dismantled, and South Africa signed the NPT in 1991.

Two developments influenced South Africa's decision. A 1988 agreement between Cuba, Angola, and the U.S. resulted in the withdrawal of 50,000 Cuban troops that had been stationed in Angola during the Cold War and supported by the Soviet Union. The risk of Soviet intervention posed by these troops in the '70s was one of the main reasons South Africa developed nuclear capability in the first place. Second, South Africa weighed the costs and benefits of joining the NPT and realized that improved relations with the world more than offset the decreasing deterrent utility from the bomb since the Cuban forces had been withdrawn and the Soviet Union no longer posed a threat.

Argentina and Brazil are two of the seven other countries that abandoned their nuclear programs before acquiring nuclear weapons. They both secretly pursued nuclear weapons capability beginning in the late '60s to early '70s. By the early '90s, both countries had given up their weapons programs and signed the NPT.

South Korea and Taiwan had secret nuclear programs in the '70s that were discovered by international intelligence. Both programs were subsequently disbanded—South Korea's in 1975 when it signed the NPT, and Taiwan's in 1988 as a result of diplomatic pressure from the U.S.

In the Middle East and North Africa, Iraq, Syria, and Libya all had active nuclear weapons programs. Iraq's nuclear program was forcibly dismantled after the Gulf War, and Libya voluntarily gave up its secret nuclear program in 2003 under the direction of Moammar Gadhafi. Syria's nuclear ambitions never progressed as far as those of its neighbors, but it is believed to have possessed enriched uranium and built a research reactor with the aid of North Korea. In 2007, Israeli airstrikes took out Syria's reactor, suspending the nuclear program indefinitely.

Nuclear Latency

When a country does not currently have nuclear weapons but has a peaceful nuclear program that could be used to produce nuclear weapons, it is said to be in a state of "nuclear latency." To build a nuclear weapon, a country must have technical knowledge and capabilities, access to materials, and a well-developed industrial sector. Of the 31 countries that possess nuclear power plants, we have identified five important countries for which the acquisition of nuclear weapons would radically impact relations with both their regional neighbors and global powers. These countries have both the technological and economic resources to develop nuclear weapons and are likely to play pivotal roles in major geopolitical events within the next decade.

Iran's nuclear ambitions led to intense negotiations with the West. In 2015, the negotiations resulted in the signing of the Joint Comprehensive Plan of Action (JCPOA), which saw Iran shelve its nuclear program for a set period of time in exchange for benefits including sanctions relief. However, if Iran were to continue enriching uranium in secret and develop a nuclear weapon despite the JCPOA, it would alter the balance of power in the region. Iran would have a new, asymmetric power relative to its Sunni rivals and force Israel to reconsider strategies that incorporate pre-emptive strikes.

Japan has large stockpiles of plutonium from civilian uses and already possesses uranium enrichment and plutonium reprocessing technologies. Estimates of Japan's breakout time range from six months to several years. Japan's alliance with the United States has thus far deterred it from developing nuclear weapons because it knows it can rely on the U.S. for defense. However, North Korea's progress in its nuclear program could drive Japan to reconsider. A nuclear Japan would threaten China's desired hegemony in the region and force it to proceed with greater caution in its actions in the South China and East China seas.

South Korea and Taiwan have advanced civilian nuclear programs and technical knowledge that could be redirected into a weapons program. They also have the need to defend against regional threats. As North Korea appears to move closer to possessing a deliverable nuclear warhead, the South Korean government has debated acquiring a nuclear weapon. Taiwan is in a similar position. Its sovereignty is threatened by mainland China, which possesses nuclear weapons. Taiwan could consider developing a nuclear weapon to discourage Chinese aspirations to fully reclaim the island. South Korea and Taiwan are concerned about escalation, however, so instead choose to rely on the nuclear guarantee provided by their alliance with the U.S.

On the other side of the world is Germany. Germany is a highly industrialized state with civilian nuclear capabilities. It is currently protected under the NATO nuclear umbrella by the U.S. and the European nuclear powers (France and the United Kingdom). It also is bound by international treaty not to pursue weapons development. However, it is not inconceivable that Germany would consider developing nuclear weapons to deter Russian aggression if it questioned America's commitment.

Conclusion

Every country has a red line, past which its security imperatives will be threatened and it will be compelled to respond with force. Without a sufficient deterrent, potential adversaries incur less risk when they test where exactly that line is. Introducing nuclear weapons into these calculations, however, forces the aggressor to proceed with caution because the risk of massive retaliation is great. This is a difficult balance to strike when the addition of nuclear weapons by one party is itself the act that breaches the security imperatives of the other.

The world's eyes are now set on North Korea for this reason: The United States is in the process of deciding whether recent developments in North Korea's nuclear program have crossed this boundary and, if they have, what force constitutes an appropriate response. Though the U.S. is not directly threatened by North Korea's nuclear weapons (based on the current understanding of its ballistic missile technology), the safety of its allies would be jeopardized by a North Korean bomb. British and French fears that the U.S. would not make good on its nuclear guarantee led to proliferation in Europe. Similarly, if the US's Asian allies question the credibility of its guarantee, the risk of nuclear proliferation in the region will grow.

"Despite an overall decrease in the number of nuclear warheads in 2020, more have been deployed with operational forces."

Global Nuclear Arsenals Are Growing

Stockholm International Peace Research Institute

In this viewpoint from the Stockholm International Peace Research Institute (SIPRI), the author argues that although there was an overall decline in nuclear arsenals between 2020 and 2021, there has been an increase in nuclear warheads in operational deployment, meaning warheads that are located on military bases or even on missiles so that they can be used quickly if necessary. Additionally, countries such as China, India, Pakistan, and North Korea seem to be interested in further developing their nuclear arsenals going forward. The Stockholm International Peace Research Institute (SIPRI) is an independent international institute dedicated to research into conflict, armaments, arms control, and disarmament.

As you read, consider the following questions:

1. According to this viewpoint, how many nuclear weapons did the nine nuclear-armed states possess in total as of 2021?
2. What percent of the global nuclear weapons do Russia and the U.S. possess?

"Global nuclear arsenals grow as states continue to modernize–New SIPRI Yearbook out now" Stockholm International Peace Research Institute (SIPRI), June 14, 2021. Reprinted by permission of Stockholm International Peace Research Institute (SIPRI).

3. Why did SIPRI have to estimate how many nuclear warheads North Korea possesses?

The Stockholm International Peace Research Institute (SIPRI) today [June 14, 2021] launches the findings of *SIPRI Yearbook 2021*, which assesses the current state of armaments, disarmament and international security. A key finding is that despite an overall decrease in the number of nuclear warheads in 2020, more have been deployed with operational forces.

Signs that Decline in Nuclear Arsenals Has Stalled

The nine nuclear-armed states—the United States, Russia, the United Kingdom, France, China, India, Pakistan, Israel and the Democratic People's Republic of Korea (North Korea)—together possessed an estimated 13,080 nuclear weapons at the start of 2021. This marked a decrease from the 13,400 that SIPRI estimated these states possessed at the beginning of 2020 (see table below).

Despite this overall decrease, the estimated number of nuclear weapons currently deployed with operational forces increased to 3825, from 3720 last year. Around 2000 of these—nearly all of which belonged to Russia or the USA—were kept in a state of high operational alert.

While the USA and Russia continued to reduce their overall nuclear weapon inventories by dismantling retired warheads in 2020, both are estimated to have had around 50 more nuclear warheads in operational deployment at the start of 2021 than a year earlier. Russia also increased its overall military nuclear stockpile by around 180 warheads, mainly due to deployment of more multi-warhead land-based intercontinental ballistic missiles (ICBMs) and sea-launched ballistic missiles (SLBMs). Both countries' deployed strategic nuclear forces remained within the limits set by the 2010 Treaty on Measures for the Further Reduction and Limitation of Strategic Offensive Arms (New START), although the treaty does not limit total nuclear warhead inventories.

"The overall number of warheads in global military stockpiles now appears to be increasing, a worrisome sign that the declining trend that has characterized global nuclear arsenals since the end of the Cold War has stalled," said Hans M. Kristensen, Associate Senior Fellow with SIPRI's Nuclear Disarmament, Arms Control and Non-proliferation Programme and Director of the Nuclear Information Project at the Federation of American Scientists (FAS). "The last-minute extension of New START by Russia and the USA in February this year was a relief, but the prospects for additional bilateral nuclear arms control between the nuclear superpowers remain poor."

Russia and the USA together possess over 90 percent of global nuclear weapons. Both have extensive and expensive programmes under way to replace and modernize their nuclear warheads, missile and aircraft delivery systems, and production facilities.

"Both Russia and the USA appear to be increasing the importance they attribute to nuclear weapons in their national security strategies," said Kristensen.

Other Nuclear-Armed States Investing in Future Capabilities

All the other seven nuclear-armed states are also either developing or deploying new weapon systems or have announced their intention to do so. The UK's "Integrated Review of Security, Defence, Development and Foreign Policy," published in early 2021, reversed a policy of reducing the country's nuclear arsenal and raised its planned ceiling for nuclear weapons from 180 to 260.

China is in the middle of a significant modernization and expansion of its nuclear weapon inventory, and India and Pakistan also appear to be expanding their nuclear arsenals.

North Korea continues to enhance its military nuclear programme as a central element of its national security strategy. While it conducted no nuclear test explosions or long-range ballistic missile tests during 2020, it continued production of fissile material and development of short- and long-range ballistic missiles.

"The entry into force of the Treaty on the Prohibition of Nuclear Weapons in early 2021 highlights the growing divide between the nuclear-armed states, which are all investing in the long-term future of their nuclear forces, and other countries that are impatient to see progress on nuclear disarmament promised by the Nuclear Non-Proliferation Treaty," said Matt Korda, Associate Researcher with SIPRI's Nuclear Disarmament, Arms Control and Non-proliferation Programme and Research Associate with the FAS Nuclear Information Project.

World Nuclear Forces, January 2021

COUNTRY	DEPLOYED WARHEADS*	OTHER WARHEADS**	TOTAL 2021	TOTAL 2020
USA	1,800	3,750	5,550	5,800
Russia	1,625	4,630	6,255	6,375
UK***	120	105	225	215
France	280	10	290	290
China	0	350	350	320
India	0	156	156	150
Pakistan	0	165	165	160
Israel	0	90	90	90
North Korea****	...	[40-50]	[40-50]	[30-40]
Total	3,825	9,255	13,080	13,400

Source: SIPRI Yearbook 2021.

*'Deployed warheads' refers to warheads placed on missiles or located on bases with operational forces.

**'Other warheads' refers to stored or reserve warheads and retired warheads awaiting dismantlement.

***The British Government declared in 2010 that its nuclear weapon inventory would not exceed 225 warheads. SIPRI estimates that the inventory remained at that number in Jan. 2021. This is a revision of previous SIPRI assessments based on new information. A planned reduction to 180 warheads by the mid 2020s was ended by a government review undertaken in 2020 and published in early 2021. The review introduced a new ceiling of 260 warheads.

ended by a government review undertaken in 2020 and published in early 2021. The review introduced a new ceiling of 260 warheads.

****The figures for North Korea are SIPRI's estimates of the number of warheads that North Korea could potentially build with the amount of fissile material it has produced. There is no publicly available evidence that North Korea has produced an operational nuclear warhead for delivery by an intercontinental-range ballistic missile, but it might have a small number of warheads for medium-range ballistic missiles. The figures for North Korea are highly uncertain and are not included in the global totals.

Notes: All estimates are approximate. SIPRI revises its world nuclear forces data each year based on new information and updates to earlier assessments. The figures for Russia and the USA do not necessarily correspond to those in their 2010 Treaty on Measures for the Further Reduction and Limitation of Strategic Offensive Arms (New START) declarations because of the treaty's counting rules. Global totals are rounded to the nearest 5 warheads.

A Mixed Outlook for Global Security and Stability

The 52nd edition of the SIPRI Yearbook reveals some negative and some hopeful developments in 2020.

"Despite outbreaks of conflict, rising military spending and of course the first year of a devastating global pandemic, overall global human security did not continue to deteriorate in 2020. The year's crumbs of comfort included a significant drop in the number of people who died in armed conflicts around the world. Unlike previous years, the international arms trade did not expand. And the Climate Action Summit made some notable—if still insufficient—progress on climate goals," said SIPRI Director Dan Smith.

In addition to its detailed coverage of nuclear arms control and non-proliferation issues, the latest edition of the SIPRI Yearbook includes insight on developments in conventional arms control in 2020; regional overviews of armed conflicts and conflict management; in-depth data and discussion on military expenditure, international arms transfers and arms production; and comprehensive coverage of efforts to counter chemical and biological security threats.

VIEWPOINT 5

> *"Nuclear anxiety has been part of the American psyche since the United States dropped atomic bombs on the Japanese cities of Hiroshima and Nagasaki in August 1945."*

Nuclear Anxiety Is Growing

Deborah Netburn

In this viewpoint, Deborah Netburn explains that during the Cold War, nuclear anxiety was a significant part of the public consciousness. There were even "duck and cover" drills in schools and other public spaces to prepare for a possible nuclear attack. However, in recent years nuclear anxiety had receded, up until Russian President Vladimir Putin threatened to use nuclear weapons as part of his attack on Ukraine in 2022. This viewpoint looks at nuclear anxiety today in comparison to Cold War nuclear anxiety. Deborah Netburn is a staff writer at the Los Angeles Times.

As you read, consider the following questions:

1. What event is cited in the viewpoint as causing a recent increase in nuclear anxiety?

2. What are the "waves" of nuclear anxiety mentioned in the viewpoint?

"New nuclear anxieties triggered by Russia-Ukraine war. 'Is anyone feeling this?'," by Deborah Netburn, Los Angeles Times, March 4, 2022. Reprinted by permission.

3. According to Francesca Giovanni, why did nuclear anxiety recede from the public imagination?

Growing up in Las Vegas in the 1980s, Glynn Walker always knew he could die in a nuclear attack.

The 43-year-old engineer remembers "duck and cover" drills in elementary school, where you dive under your desk in the event of an air raid, and basement fallout shelters in churches and gymnasiums with radiation-warning signs on their doors.

"We had the nuclear test sites, Nellis Air Force Base, the Hoover Dam," he said, referring to Nevada landmarks that likely were in the crosshairs of Soviet military strategists. "We knew we'd be a target," he said.

The prospect of nuclear war also permeated popular culture at the time, as it had done during the initial nuclear era of the 1940s, '50s and '60s. Movies like "WarGames," "Red Dawn" and "The Day After" played on TV. Pro-wrestling hero Hulk Hogan battled the villainous Russian Nikolai Volkoff right after Saturday morning cartoons. "99 Luftballoons," a pop song about an accidentally triggered Armageddon, by the German new wave band Nena, was a radio hit in the early 1980s.

"I can remember riding my bike through the desert as a kid and thinking one day this whole valley will be a radioactive hole," Walker said. "I didn't panic about it. It was just the way it was."

As the years passed, Walker stopped worrying about nuclear bombs as other threats emerged: terrorism, the war in Iraq, climate change. But the old anxieties came flooding back last week as Russian President Vladimir Putin launched a massive military invasion of Ukraine, while warning potential foes who intervened of "consequences greater than any you have ever faced in history," and putting his nuclear forces on high alert.

Walker doesn't think nuclear war over Ukraine is likely. "My hope is there are some guardrails or he's playing chicken," he said of Russia's pugilist-in-chief.

And yet, like other Americans, some for the first time in years, he's found himself fantasizing about what would happen if a nuclear bomb went off near his home in the Atlanta suburbs, several miles from the nearest city.

"This time I'm thinking I won't be eviscerated, instead I'll be left to slowly die of radiation poisoning," he said.

That brings him no comfort.

"I don't want to watch my children die and I don't want to let them see me die either," he said.

Experts say that Putin has little to gain from starting a nuclear war, but his recent rhetoric has stirred up long-buried fears in generations of Americans who grew up believing nuclear annihilation was not just possible, but practically inevitable.

"All it took was one guy basically saying, 'OK, I'm putting my guys on nuclear alert,' and all of a sudden all the movies in our head are back,'" said David Greenwald, a psychologist and author of the 1987 book "No Reason to Talk About It: Families Confront the Nuclear Taboo." Putin "brought this stuff out of the closet."

Nuclear anxiety has been part of the American psyche since the United States dropped atomic bombs on the Japanese cities of Hiroshima and Nagasaki in August 1945. What before had seemed like science fiction suddenly became reality: Humanity was armed with the power to destroy civilization.

Children, struggling to process what most grown-ups could barely comprehend, let alone deal with psychologically, were especially impacted.

"There was a lot of research that showed the youth at that time experienced deep fear and anxiety that adults could no longer protect them from adult things," said Spencer Weart, a science historian and author of "The Rise of Nuclear Fear." "People who joined the counterculture in the '60s will tell you it was 'duck and cover' and hiding from 'the bomb' that convinced them we had to change the system."

The fear came in waves, peaking in 1962 during the Cuban Missile Crisis and again in the early 1980s because both Soviet and

U.S leadership seemed unpredictable, if not bent on confrontation. But even as global warming supplanted atomic Armageddon as the most likely destroyer of civilizations, the threat of nuclear war never went away entirely.

"It receded from the public imagination in part because there were other problems that came to the fore, but we still live in a world of nuclear weapons," said Francesca Giovanni, executive director of the Project on Managing the Atom at Harvard. "It's always been in the background."

For many adults who've lived their entire lives in the shadow of "the Bomb," the sense of deja vu is palpable.

As a child in New York City in the 1960s, Victor Narro remembers feeling comforted whenever he saw a sign indicating a fallout shelter—three yellow triangles in a black circle. "As a kid I held that image as a sacred image of safety," he said. "That was the indoctrination."

His family immigrated from Peru to New York City in the '60s, when he was 4 years old. When he started kindergarten the following year his teachers told him the city would likely be the first target in a nuclear war—that's why his class had to do so many drills.

"They were always leading us to different parts of the playground," he said.

In college, Narro became a student activist and put a lot energy into trying to dismantle the arms race. But the work felt hopeless to him and he came to believe he would not make it out of the 1980s alive. He relied on his Catholic faith to help him cope. "I remember praying a lot," he said.

The end of Ronald Reagan's presidency brought Narro some relief, as did the dismantling of the Soviet Union in 1991.

"By the early 1990s, I started feeling like it was behind me," he said. "I knew there would always be nuclear weapons, but the end of the Cold War felt like the end of the policy of destruction from both sides to maintain peace."

This last week however, the old feelings of fear and hopelessness resurfaced.

When Putin started talking about nuclear weapons, Narro posted a fallout shelter sign to social media. "I was like, 'Is anyone feeling this?'" he said. "I wanted to re-create that space of safety."

For Kim Lachance Shandrow, 46, a freelance journalist in Long Beach, the week's events brought back memories of a particularly frightening music video from the 1980s, Genesis' "Land of Confusion."

"I didn't see any of the nuclear war movies, but I watched MTV like a maniac and recorded videos as if they would never be shown again," she said.

Lachance Shandrow wasn't a huge Genesis fan, but "Land of Confusion" was one of the videos she taped and watched over and over again. It stars a creepy Ronald Reagan puppet in the midst of a fever dream. In the final moments of the video, he reaches out from a brass bed to call a nurse to bring him a glass of water. Instead of pressing the red button marked "Nurse," he pushes the one just above it marked "Nuke." The video ends with a fiery mushroom cloud.

"We were painfully aware that could happen anytime, anywhere," she said.

The video was released in 1986, the same year that Lachance Shandrow remembers visiting the Trump Hotel and Casino in Atlantic City, N.J., with her family. Her parents left her and her sister in the hotel room while they went downstairs to drink and gamble. It was April 26, the day the nuclear reactor at Chernobyl in Ukraine (then part of the Soviet Union) exploded, and Lachance Shandrow and her sister watched the news all day long.

"I was 11 and that was the period in my life when I started to question Catholicism and my Catholic school experience," Lachance Shandrow said. "The Genesis video was a big video for me, and Chernobyl was life-changing."

Memories of the Chernobyl disaster were kindled early Friday, when a fire broke out at Ukraine's gigantic Zaporizhzhia nuclear complex amid the fighting, and it was seized by Russian forces.

While pop culture has extracted some catharsis from our nuclear anxieties over the decades—Stanley Kubrick's "Dr. Strangelove or:

How I Learned to Stop Worrying and Love the Bomb" (1964) is a masterpiece of fission-reaction gallows humor—a handful of books have tried to warn about the possible fate of the earth if humankind isn't careful.

The last chapter of planetary scientist Carl Sagan's best-selling classic "Cosmos," published in 1980, is a plea to the people of Earth to wake up to the danger of nuclear weapons.

"From an extraterrestrial perspective, our global civilization is clearly on the edge of failure in the most important task it faces," he wrote. "To preserve the lives and well-being of the citizens of the planet."

Over the next decade, he and his wife, "Cosmos" co-author Ann Druyan, led protests at nuclear test sites in Nevada, where they were arrested several times.

Over time, they felt they were successful in helping to bring public attention to the cause of de-escalation and disarmament. The number of nuclear warheads in the world had been reduced by 40,000 from the height of the Cold War to the end of the Obama administration.

"Someone was listening," Druyan said in an interview this week from her home in Ithaca, N.Y.

In the 1990s, the couple turned their attention to climate change, which appeared to be moving faster than earlier models had predicted.

Druyan said she understood the shock that so many felt when Putin put the world back on nuclear notice.

"Here we are in a situation we have not been thinking about because we had other fish to fry," she said. "When we look at the destruction of the entire Earth, we were thinking the feedback mechanism speeding up was the most urgent problem, and suddenly the subject has been changed."

Periodical and Internet Sources Bibliography

The following articles have been selected to supplement the diverse views presented in this chapter.

Doug Bandow, "Weighing a Nuclear Threat," *American Conservative*, January 19, 2023. https://www.theamericanconservative.com/weighing-a-nuclear-threat/.

Julian E. Barnes and David E. Sanger, "Fears of Russian Nuclear Weapons Use Have Diminished, but Could Reemerge," *New York Times,* February 3, 2023. https://www.nytimes.com/2023/02/03/us/politics/russia-nuclear-weapons.html.

William Burr and Jeffrey Kimball, "Nuclear Threats and Alerts: Looking at the Cold War Background," Arms Control Association, April 2022. https://www.armscontrol.org/act/2022-04/features/nuclear-threats-alerts-looking-cold-war-background.

Karen Feldscher, "With Conflict in Ukraine, Threat of Nuclear War Is Back 'Front and Center,'" Harvard School of Public Health, October 18, 2022. https://www.hsph.harvard.edu/news/features/with-conflict-in-ukraine-threat-of-nuclear-war-is-back-front-and-center/.

Fred Kaplan, "Apocalypse Averted," *Slate*, February 18, 2021. https://slate.com/news-and-politics/2021/02/able-archer-nuclear-war-reagan.html.

Tom Nichols and Kevin Townsend, "*Radio Atlantic*: This Is Not Your Parents' Cold War," *Atlantic,* February 17, 2023. https://www.theatlantic.com/politics/archive/2023/02/this-is-not-your-parents-cold-war/673119/.

Gideon Rachman, "The Nuclear Threats that Hang Over the World," *Financial Times*, October 31, 2022. https://www.ft.com/content/f3dce448-a7e4-4fbe-80a4-d317af4b8317.

J. Peter Scoblic, "The Russian Nuclear Threat, Explained," *Vox*, October 5, 2022. https://www.vox.com/2022/10/5/23387707/russia-ukraine-nuclear-weapons-tactical-us-nato.

Francine Uenuma, "The 1983 Military Drill That Nearly Sparked Nuclear War with the Soviets," *Smithsonian Magazine*, April 27, 2022. https://www.smithsonianmag.com/history/the-1983-

military-drill-that-nearly-sparked-nuclear-war-with-the-soviets-180979980/.

Christina Wilkie, "Putin's Nuclear Threats Move Doomsday Clock Closest Ever to Armageddon, Atomic Scientists Say," CNBC, January 24, 2023. https://www.cnbc.com/2023/01/24/putins-nuclear-threats-move-doomsday-clock-closest-ever-to-armageddon-atomic-scientists-say.html.

OPPOSING
VIEWPOINTS®
SERIES

CHAPTER 2

Should the United States Possess Nuclear Weapons?

Chapter Preface

As of 2021 (the most recent data available at the time of publication), the United States possessed 5,550 nuclear warheads.[1] Despite the fact that this is considerably less than its peak in 1967, when the U.S. had 31,255 nuclear weapons in its stockpile, it remains the country with the largest nuclear arsenal.[2] Whether this fact is beneficial or detrimental to the country's sense of security is a hotly debated topic.

On the one hand, proponents of maintaining a large nuclear arsenal argue that it is essential for nuclear deterrence, or keeping rogue countries and non-state actors such as terrorists in check, since they assert that knowing that the U.S. is capable of intense retaliation is enough to prevent these countries and groups from making an attack. Additionally, the United States' nuclear arsenal does not just offer protection for itself, but to its allies that do not possess nuclear weapons as well. This concept is known as the "nuclear umbrella," and it means that the U.S. will defend non-nuclear allies using its nuclear weapons in the event of an attack. The U.S. has nuclear umbrella agreements with other countries in the North Atlantic Treaty Organization (NATO), South Korea, Australia, and Japan.[3]

However, those who support nuclear disarmament argue that the U.S.—and every other country—will never truly be safe as long as nuclear weapons exist. They claim that even if the U.S. has the largest nuclear stockpile, any nuclear conflict will likely result in the deaths of billions of people.[4] Furthermore, maintaining a nuclear stockpile is extremely expensive. According to a report from the Defense Department and the Energy Department's National Nuclear Security Administration (NNSA), the U.S.'s nuclear arsenal will cost $634 billion between 2021 and 2030.[5] Some argue that this money would be much better used if allocated to other issues.

The viewpoints in this chapter consider perspectives on both sides of the debate over whether the U.S. should possess nuclear weapons. They consider the political, economic, and security implications of this question to offer a clearer understanding of the issue.

Notes

1. "Global nuclear arsenals grow as states continue to modernize–New SIPRI Yearbook out now," Stockholm International Peace Research Institute (SIPRI), June 14, 2021. https://www.sipri.org/media/press-release/2021/global-nuclear-arsenals-grow-states-continue-modernize-new-sipri-yearbook-out-now.
2. "Nuclear Stockpile Transparency," National Nuclear Security Administration. https://www.energy.gov/nnsa/nuclear-stockpile-transparency.
3. Gregory Kulacki "The U.S. Doesn't Need to Worry About Japan (or Any Other Ally) Going Nuclear," the *Diplomat*, February 5, 2021. https://thediplomat.com/2021/02/the-us-doesnt-need-to-worry-about-japan-or-any-other-ally-going-nuclear/.
4. Max Roser, "Nuclear Weapons: Why Reducing the Risk of Nuclear War Should Be a Key Concern of Our Generation," Our World in Data, March 3, 2022. https://ourworldindata.org/nuclear-weapons-risk.
5. Kingston Reif and Shannon Bugos, "Projected Cost of U.S. Nuclear Arsenal Rises," Arms Control Association, June 2021. https://www.armscontrol.org/act/2021-06/news/projected-cost-us-nuclear-arsenal-rises.

"By building a robust nuclear force, America's losses in a nuclear war— though extraordinary—will be less than its adversaries'."

The U.S. Must Maintain a Large Nuclear Arsenal

Zachary Keck

In this viewpoint, Zachary Keck examines an argument Georgetown professor Matthew Kroenig makes in his book The Logic of American Strategy *that asserts that it is necessary for the United States to maintain nuclear superiority in order to effectively protect its national security goals. According to this viewpoint, this stance goes against what most academics believe to be true, but Kroenig asserts that having a large nuclear arsenal would allow the U.S. to take more strategic risks in a nuclear conflict because they'd be able to take out opponents' arsenals. Zachary Keck is a foreign policy professional with expertise in the Indo-Pacific, nuclear weapons issues, and defense.*

As you read, consider the following questions:

1. According to this viewpoint, what did Thomas Schelling say about mutually assured destruction?

"This Is Why America Needs Tons of Nuclear Weapons," by Zachary Keck, National Interest, May 4, 2018. Reprinted by permission.

2. As cited in this viewpoint, how much destruction does Matthew Kroenig think could be done by a Russian first-strike nuclear attack?

3. What are some of the emerging military technologies Keck mentions toward the end of the viewpoint?

There is a widely acknowledged gap between policy making and academic theory. As Paul Nitze once observed:

> Most of what has been written and taught under the heading of "political science" by Americans since World War II has been contrary to experience and common sense. It has also been of limited value, if not counterproductive, as a guide to the actual conduct of policy.

This gap is especially pronounced in the realm of nuclear strategy. In academia, nuclear scholars have consistently argued that nuclear-armed states only need a limited number of warheads to maintain a secure second-strike capability, and building larger arsenals is of no utility. During the Cold War, however, the Soviet Union and United States built tens of thousands of weapons, and Moscow and Washington still maintain arsenals well in excess of what academics believe is necessary. In seeking to explain this gap, most scholars have fallen back on the argument that the superpowers are simply acting "illogical" when it comes to nuclear strategy.

Matthew Kroenig seeks to bridge this gap in his new book, *The Logic of American Strategy: Why Strategic Superiority Matters.* A professor at Georgetown University, Kroenig often takes controversial positions and challenges the conventional wisdom, especially the conventional wisdom in the Ivory Tower. In doing so, he makes his points so persuasively that even his staunchest critics are forced to grapple with his arguments.

The Logic of American Strategy is arguably Kroenig's most ambitious project yet. The book challenges the conventional wisdom on U.S. nuclear strategy but does so from a position firmly grounded in the work that came before it. Thus, Kroenig accepts that a secure second-strike capability is sufficient for deterring most conventional attacks, but "argues that military nuclear advantages above and beyond a secure, second-strike capability can contribute to a state's national security goals." Most notably, his "superiority-brinkmanship synthesis theory" contends that by building a robust nuclear posture—"with capabilities designed to limit damage in the event of nuclear war"—the United States enhances its ability to take risks in nuclear crises. That is because America has counterforce capabilities—i.e., those that can take out an adversary's nuclear arsenal—that reduce the level of destruction it would suffer in a nuclear attack.

Again, this is rooted in the pioneering work of intellectual giants like Thomas Schelling. As Schelling demonstrated, in a world characterized by Mutually Assured Destruction, countries are less likely to fight wars. In their place, countries compete through brinkmanship, where each side takes increasingly risky actions in an effort to get the other side to back down. Brinkmanship is a battle of resolve, and most theorists believe that whichever side has greater interests at stake will demonstrate more resolve. That is, they will be willing to take the most risky actions in order to achieve their ends. This presents a paradox for the United States. As the only country that provides extended deterrence over its allies in theatres like Europe and Asia, it almost always has less at stake than adversaries like Russia and China. Thus, if resolve is simply a matter of which side has greater stakes at risk, America should lose every time.

Why doesn't this happen, then? Kroenig argues that resolve is about more than what interests are at stake. Similar to Daryl Press's theory on credibility, Kroenig argues that resolve is better calculated as a combination of the stakes involved and each state's capabilities. By building a robust nuclear force, America's losses in a nuclear war—though extraordinary—will be less than its adversaries. This makes U.S. leaders more willing to gamble in nuclear crises than they otherwise would be. As Kroenig puts it:

Leaders in nuclear superior states still badly want to avoid a nuclear exchange, but because the costs of a nuclear exchange are relatively lower, we should expect that they will be willing, on average, to hazard a higher risk of disaster than their nuclear inferior opponents, making them more likely to ultimately win nuclear crises.

To demonstrate this logic, Kroenig does what few modern nuclear scholars bother doing—namely, mapping out how a nuclear war might unfold. While this was common practice during the Cold War—and another area where Kroenig is building on the work of prior nuclear scholars—few contemporaries are comfortable with thinking the unthinkable (at least in the public domain). For them, distinctions fail to matter when one's talking about something as destructive as nuclear warfare. Kroenig does not deny that any nuclear war would be horrific, but contends that there are meaningful differences in scale. For instance, the United States would undeniably suffer less from a Chinese nuclear first strike than a Russian one. "To argue otherwise," Kroenig writes, "one would have to maintain that the destruction of 86 US cities, including Honolulu, New Orleans, and Pittsburgh, does not matter. One would also have to argue that the loss of 20 million American lives is inconsequential. Such a position is untenable."

In what is likely the most controversial chapter of the book, Kroenig shows the enormous differences in lives lost when the United States has a robust nuclear force that is capable of carrying out counterforce strikes. Consider the differences between a Russian first and second strike under current conditions. In a first strike, Moscow could destroy 131 American cities with an estimated 70 million casualties (assuming it was also trying to reduce America's ability to retaliate). If Russia's arsenal had already been targeted by a U.S. counterforce attack, its second strike would hit twelve cities and cause 28 million casualties. These numbers would be a lot different if the United States implemented unilateral nuclear reductions, as some have advocated. In one of the most interesting points in the book, Kroenig points out that if the United

States eliminated its ICBM force—as many now advocate—it would free up more Russian nuclear warheads to target U.S. cities. In fact, by Kroenig's calculations, there would be more American casualties in a Russian second strike with a reduced U.S. arsenal than in a first strike under current conditions. Instead of the 70 million casualties in a first strike under current conditions, a Russian second strike with a reduced U.S. arsenal would cause 82 million casualties. That's because more of Moscow's arsenal would survive a first strike and also it wouldn't have to devote many warheads to U.S. nuclear targets like ICBMs.

Even if logically sound, social science theories count for little if they don't explain the world. In this vein, Kroenig devotes a chapter to conducting qualitative and quantitative tests of his superiority-brinkmanship synthesis theory. The quantitative analysis finds that "nuclear superior states are over ten times more likely than nuclear inferior states to achieve their basic goals in international crises." Interestingly, he finds that nuclear superior states have never faced compellent threats. "Nuclear superiority deter compellence," Kroenig writes. Many of these findings depend on how one interprets and codes events. After all, Todd S. Sechser and Matthew Fuhrmann's recent book found that nuclear weapons are poor tools for coercion. There is little doubt that some U.S. presidents believed that nuclear superiority—or a lack therefore of—was hugely important. Richard Nixon and Henry Kissinger often bemoaned how the Soviet Union achieving nuclear parity constrained their freedom of action. Nonetheless, they still attempted nuclear coercion and it's unclear whether their assessments were correct.

After testing his theory, Kroenig provides rebuttals to what he believes critics will say about the dangers and costs of striving for nuclear superiority. Many of these will be controversial but, as usual, persuasive enough that they will have to be engaged by critics. One issue that could have received more attention in the book is how emerging military technologies could impact the relevancy of nuclear superiority. For instance, advances in the accuracy of missiles, the development of hypersonics and perhaps even cyber weapons could make effective nonnuclear counterforce strikes more effective. At the very least, these will have to be part of the strategic balance leaders consider in assessing their own and adversaries' capabilities.

In final analysis, *The Logic of American Nuclear Strategy* makes an important contribution to the academic literature while also being highly relevant and extremely readable for policymakers and the general public. In this way, Kroenig's work itself embodies bridging the academic and policy worlds.

"The world has learned that nuclear armament is not the one-way street that it was once believed to be. Disarmament is possible."

Nuclear Disarmament Is the Only Way to Prevent Nuclear War

Max Roser

In this viewpoint, Max Roser asserts that the threat of global devastation through nuclear fallout and a nuclear winter makes the prospect of a nuclear war a major cause for concern. In fact, Roser asserts that in the event of a nuclear winter, billions of people would likely die. Although nuclear stockpiles have shrunk since the Cold War, the only way to fully eliminate this threat is complete nuclear disarmament. Despite the belief that countries would never actually use nuclear weapons because of mutually assured destruction, there have been a number of alarming close calls. However, Roser argues that there are ways to promote peace and reduce the risk of nuclear war. Dr. Max Roser is founder and director of Our World in Data, a scientific online publication.

As you read, consider the following questions:

1. According to this viewpoint, what is a nuclear winter? What could be the effects of a nuclear winter?
2. What is the "balance of terror"?

"Nuclear weapons: Why reducing the risk of nuclear war should be a key concern of our generation," by Dr. Max Roser, Our World in Data, March 3, 2022. https://ourworldindata.org/nuclear-weapons-risk. Licensed under CC BY 4.0 International.

3. According to Roser, what are some of the ways the risk of nuclear war can be reduced?

The shockwave and heat that the detonation of a single nuclear weapon creates can end the lives of millions of people immediately.

But even larger is the devastation that would follow a nuclear war.

The first reason for this is nuclear fallout. Radioactive dust from the detonating bombs rises up into the atmosphere and spreads out over large areas of the world from where it falls down and causes deadly levels of radiation.

The second reason is less widely known. But this consequence—"nuclear winter" and the worldwide famine that would follow—is now "believed to be the most serious consequence of nuclear war.

Cities that are attacked by nuclear missiles burn at such an intensity that they create their own wind system, a firestorm: hot air above the burning city ascends and is replaced by air that rushes in from all directions. The storm-force winds fan the flames and create immense heat.

From this firestorm large columns of smoke and soot rise up above the burning cities and travel all the way up to the stratosphere. There it spreads around the planet and blocks the sun's light. At that great height—far above the clouds—it cannot be rained out, meaning that it will remain there for years, darkening the sky and thereby drying and chilling the planet.

The nuclear winter that would follow a large-scale nuclear war is expected to lead to temperature declines of 20 or even 30 degrees Celsius (60–86° F) in many of the world's agricultural regions—including much of Eurasia and North America. Nuclear winter would cause a "nuclear famine." The world's food production would fail and billions of people would starve.

These consequences—nuclear fallout and nuclear winter leading to famine—mean that the destruction caused by nuclear weapons is not contained to the battlefield. It would not just harm the attacked country. Nuclear war would devastate all countries, including the attacker.

The possibility of global devastation is what makes the prospect of nuclear war so very terrifying. And it is also why nuclear weapons are so unattractive for warfare. A weapon that can lead to self-destruction is not a weapon that can be used strategically.

U.S. President Reagan put it in clear words at the height of the Cold War:

> *A nuclear war cannot be won and must never be fought. The only value in our two nations possessing nuclear weapons is to make sure they will never be used. But then would it not be better to do away with them entirely?*

Nuclear Stockpiles Have Been Reduced, but the Risk Remains High

40 years after Reagan's words, the Cold War is over and nuclear stockpiles have been reduced considerably.

The world has learned that nuclear armament is not the one-way street that it was once believed to be. Disarmament is possible.

But there are still almost ten thousand nuclear weapons distributed among nine countries on our planet, at least. Each of these weapons can cause enormous destruction; many are much larger than the ones that the U.S. dropped on Hiroshima and Nagasaki.

Collectively these weapons are immensely destructive. The nuclear winter scenario outlined above would kill billions of people—*billions*—in the years that follow a large-scale nuclear war, even if it was fought "only" with today's reduced stockpiles.

It is unclear whether humanity as a species could possibly survive a full-scale nuclear war with the current stockpiles. A nuclear war might well be humanity's final war.

Close Calls: Instances that Threatened to Push the "Balance of Terror" Out of Balance and Into War

The "balance of terror" is the idea that all involved political leaders are so scared of nuclear war that they never launch a nuclear attack.

If this is achievable at all, it can only be achieved if all nuclear powers keep their weapons in check. This is because the balance is vulnerable to accidents: a nuclear bomb that detonates accidentally—or even just a false alarm, with no weapons even involved—can trigger nuclear retaliation because several countries keep their nuclear weapons on "launch on warning"; in response to a warning, their leaders can decide within minutes whether they want to launch a retaliatory strike.

For the balance of terror to be a balance, all parties need to be in control at all times. This however is not the case.

The risk of nuclear war might well be low—because neither side would want to fight such a war that would have such awful consequences for everyone on the planet. But there is a risk that the kinds of technical errors and accidents listed here could lead accidentally to the use of nuclear weapons, as a nuclear power can incorrectly come to believe that they are under attack.

This is why false alarms, errors, and close calls are so crucial to monitor: they are the incidents that can push the "balance of terror" out of balance and into war.

Accidents and errors are of course not the only possible path that could lead to the use of nuclear weapons. There is the risk of a terribly irresponsible person leading a country possessing nuclear weapons. There is the risk of nuclear terrorism, possibly after a terrorist organization steals weapons. There is the possibility that hackers can take control of the nuclear chain of command. And there is the possibility that several of these factors play a role at the same time.

How to Reduce the Risk of Nuclear War

An escalating conflict between nuclear powers—but also an accident, a hacker, a terrorist, or an irresponsible leader—could lead to the detonation of nuclear weapons.

Those risks only go to zero if all nuclear weapons are removed from the world. I believe this is what humanity should work toward, but it is exceedingly hard to achieve, at least in the short term. It is therefore important to see that there are additional ways that can reduce the chance of the world suffering the horrors of nuclear war.

A More Peaceful World

Many world regions in which our ancestors fought merciless wars over countless generations are extraordinarily peaceful in our times. The rise of democracy, international trade, diplomacy, and a cultural attitude shift against the glorification of war are some of the drivers credited for this development.

Making the world a more peaceful place will reduce the risk of nuclear confrontation. Efforts that reduce the chance of any war reduce the chance of nuclear war.

Nuclear Treaties

Several non-proliferation treaties have been key in achieving the large reduction of nuclear stockpiles. However, key treaties—like the Intermediate-Range Nuclear Forces (INF) Treaty between the U.S. and Russia—have been suspended and additional agreements could be reached.

The UN Treaty on the Prohibition of Nuclear Weapons, which became effective in 2021, is a recent development in this direction.

Smaller Nuclear Stockpiles

Reducing the stockpiles further is seen as an important and achievable goal by experts.

It is considered achievable because smaller stockpiles would still provide the deterrence benefits from nuclear weapons. And it is important as it reduces the risk of accidents and the chance that a possible nuclear war would end civilization.

Better Monitoring, Better Control

The risk can be further reduced by efforts to better control nuclear weapons—so that close calls occur less frequently. Similarly better monitoring systems would reduce the chance of false alarms.

Taking nuclear weapons off "hair-trigger alert" would reduce the risk that any accident that does occur can rapidly spiral out of control. And a well-resourced International Atomic Energy Agency can verify that the agreements in the treaties are met.

Better Public Understanding, Global Relations, and Culture

Finally I also believe that it will help to see clearly that billions of us share the same goal. None of us wants to live through a nuclear war, none of us wants to die in one. As Reagan said, a nuclear war cannot be won and it would be better to do away with these weapons entirely.

A generation ago a broad and highly visible societal movement pursued the goal of nuclear disarmament. These efforts were to a good extent successful. But since then, this goal has unfortunately lost much of the attention it once received—and this is despite the fact that things have not fundamentally changed: the world still possesses weapons that could kill billions. I wish it was a more prominent concern in our generation so that more young people would set themselves the goal to make the world safe from nuclear weapons.

Conclusion

I believe some dangers are exaggerated—for example, I believe that the fear of terrorist attacks is often wildly out of proportion with the actual risk. But when it comes to nuclear weapons I believe the opposite is true.

There are many today who hardly give nuclear conflict a thought and I think this is a big mistake.

For eight decades people have been producing nuclear weapons. Several countries have dedicated vast sums of money to their construction. And now we live in a world in which these weapons endanger our entire civilization and our future.

These destructive weapons are perhaps the clearest example that technology and innovation are not only forces for good, they can also enable catastrophic destruction.

Without the Second World War and the Cold War, the world might have never developed these weapons and we might find the idea that anyone could possibly build such weapons unimaginable. But this is not the world we live in. We live in a world with weapons of enormous destructiveness and we have to see the risks that they pose to all of us and find ways to reduce them.

I hope that there are many in the world today who take on the challenge to make the world more peaceful and to reduce the risk from nuclear weapons. The goal has to be that humanity never ends up using this most destructive technology that we ever developed.

> "The estimate is 28 percent higher than the previous 10-year projection released in 2019 and could exacerbate concerns about the necessity and the sustainability of the current nuclear modernization effort."

Maintaining a Large Nuclear Arsenal Is Too Expensive

Kingston Reif and Shannon Bugos

In this viewpoint, Kingston Reif and Shannon Bugos examine a 2021 report from the Congressional Budget Office (CBO) on the projected costs of sustaining and modernizing the United States' nuclear arsenal in the coming years. According to the CBO, between 2019 and 2021 alone the 10-year estimate increased by 28 percent. The CBO report considers costs associated with nuclear delivery vehicles, warheads, and related infrastructure from programs operated by the National Nuclear Security Administration (NNSA), which is managed and funded by the Defense Department and Energy Department. According to the authors, the rising costs of maintaining and modernizing the nuclear arsenal raises questions on whether it's necessary to do this. Kingston Reif is the Deputy Assistant Secretary of Defense for Threat Reduction and Arms Control at the Pentagon. Shannon Bugos is a senior policy analyst at the Arms Control Association.

"Projected Cost of U.S. Nuclear Arsenal Rises," by Kingston Reif and Shannon Bugos, Arms Control Association, June 2021. Reprinted by permission.

As you read, consider the following questions:

1. According to this viewpoint, how much is the U.S. projected to spend on its nuclear arsenal between 2021 and 2030?
2. What percent of total national defense spending does the Congressional Budget Office (CBO) estimate will go toward the nuclear arsenal between 2021 and 2030?
3. According to this viewpoint, how does the CBO make its projections?

The United States will spend a total of $634 billion over the next 10 years to sustain and modernize its nuclear arsenal, according to the latest projection by the Congressional Budget Office (CBO). The estimate is 28 percent higher than the previous 10-year projection released in 2019 and could exacerbate concerns about the necessity and the sustainability of the current nuclear modernization effort amid what experts predict will likely be a flat defense budget in the coming years.

The CBO report, published May 24, includes the projected costs to sustain and modernize U.S. delivery vehicles, warheads, and their associated infrastructure across a range of programs that are managed by the Defense Department and the Energy Department's semiautonomous National Nuclear Security Administration (NNSA). The report estimates that the $634 billion in planned spending in fiscal years 2021–2030 will consume 6.0–8.5 percent of projected total spending on national defense during those years.

The 2019 CBO report had forecast total U.S. spending on nuclear forces at $494 billion through 2028 and estimated that the annual cost during those years would be 5–7 percent of the national defense budget.

Of the $140 billion increase in spending identified in the 2021 report, the CBO attributed 36 percent, or about $50 billion, to an increase in spending on nuclear weapons during the eight years, from 2021 to 2028, that overlap in both estimates.

Another 50 percent or so of the increase results from inflation and from the fact that the 2021 report begins and ends two years later than the previous projection, the CBO calculated. The other 15 percent reflects the estimated cost of growth beyond projected amounts.

The percentage increase of the nuclear weapons budget administered by the Energy Department is "substantially higher" than that for the Defense Department, the report said, with Energy Department costs "projected to total $229 billion, or 36 percent more than CBO estimated in 2019, whereas [Defense Department] costs are projected to total $406 billion, or 25 percent more than CBO estimated in 2019."

Congress appropriated $15.4 billion for NNSA nuclear weapons activities in fiscal year 2021, a nearly 25 percent increase above the previous year's appropriation. Modernization costs for nuclear command, control, communications, and early-warning systems increased by $17 billion, to $94 billion, over 10 years in the latest CBO report.

Within the triad of nuclear delivery systems, projected spending on the U.S. fleet of ballistic missile submarines increased significantly, with the CBO putting the total price tag at $145 billion over 10 years, which is a $38 billion increase from the previous CBO estimate. The CBO attributed some of the increase to higher operating costs for the current fleet and plans to operate some of the submarines longer than initially planned.

The cost of U.S. intercontinental ballistic missiles is projected to grow to $82 billion over 10 years, $21 billion more than the 2019 projection. The CBO said that was due primarily to the difference in time periods covered by the reports.

In addition, the CBO report estimates that the United States will spend $53 billion over the next 10 years on strategic bombers. The CBO notes that the estimate only covers a quarter of the costs of the B-52 bomber and the new B-21 bomber because the rest of the costs are assigned to the bombers' conventional, not nuclear, mission. If the full cost of B-52 and B-21 bombers were included, the total cost of nuclear forces would be $711 billion, including cost growth.

CBO projections are based on the plans reflected in the fiscal year 2021 budget requests that the Defense and Energy departments under the Trump administration submitted in February 2020, "provided those plans did not change or experience any cost growth or schedule delays." The CBO also assumed that the Pentagon would move forward with directives listed in the 2018 Nuclear Posture Review, such as the fielding of a new sea-launched cruise missile (SLCM), although this program is believed to be under review by the Biden administration.

The CBO report said that the estimate of the costs of the SLCM and its warhead of about $10 billion from 2021 to 2030 "is highly uncertain; in fact, it is still not clear whether the program will be pursued at all and, if so, what the design and development schedule will be."

*"As long as nuclear weapons
exist, NATO will remain a
nuclear alliance."*

Nuclear Deterrence Is at the Core of NATO's Defense Policy

NATO

In this viewpoint from the North Atlantic Treaty Organization (NATO), the author explains why nuclear weapons play an important role in NATO's defense and deterrence policies. Although the viewpoint asserts that NATO ultimately supports nonproliferation and disarmament, as long as nations outside of NATO possess nuclear weapons, NATO will have to possess them as well. Nuclear weapons help guarantee the security of all the allies in NATO. In response to Russia's war on Ukraine, NATO asserts that building up a stronger nuclear program for defense and deterrence is necessary. NATO is an intergovernmental military alliance made up of 30 independent member countries, including the United States.

As you read, consider the following questions:

1. According to this viewpoint, what is the basis for NATO's current nuclear policy?
2. What is the fundamental purpose for NATO's nuclear forces?

"NATO's nuclear deterrence policy and forces", NATO, July 6, 2022. Reprinted by Permission. © NATO

3. How much has NATO reduced its nuclear arsenal since the Cold War?

Nuclear weapons are a core component of NATO's overall capabilities for deterrence and defence, alongside conventional and missile defence forces. NATO is committed to arms control, disarmament and non-proliferation, but as long as nuclear weapons exist, it will remain a nuclear alliance.

NATO's Nuclear Deterrence Policy

The fundamental purpose of NATO's nuclear capability is to preserve peace, prevent coercion and deter aggression. As long as nuclear weapons exist, NATO will remain a nuclear alliance. NATO's goal is a safer world for all; the Alliance seeks to create the security environment for a world without nuclear weapons.

NATO's current nuclear policy is based on two public documents agreed by all Allies:

- The 2022 Strategic Concept
- The 2012 Deterrence and Defence Posture Review

The 2022 Strategic Concept, adopted by Allied Heads of State and Government at the NATO Summit in Madrid sets out the Alliance's core tasks and principles, including deterrence. It states that NATO's deterrence and defence posture is based on an appropriate mix of nuclear, conventional and missile defence capabilities, complemented by space and cyber capabilities.

The Alliance reaffirms the imperative to ensure the broadest possible participation by Allies concerned in the agreed nuclear burden-sharing arrangements to demonstrate Alliance unity and resolve.

The Deterrence and Defence Posture Review (DDPR) was endorsed by Allied Heads of State and Government at the NATO Chicago Summit in May 2012. The DDPR stressed that the fundamental purpose of Alliance nuclear forces is deterrence, which is essentially a political function. While the Alliance focuses on the maintenance of effective deterrence, political control of nuclear weapons will be kept under all circumstances and nuclear planning and consultation within the Alliance will be in accordance with political guidance.

NATO continues to affirm the importance of nuclear deterrence in light of evolving challenges. Allies have reiterated this principle at successive summit meetings since 2014 (the 2014 Wales Summit, the 2016 Warsaw Summit, and the 2018 and 2021 Brussels Summits), including the Madrid Summit in 2022, where Heads of State and Government agreed the Strategic Concept, which states that: "NATO will take all necessary steps to ensure the credibility, effectiveness, safety and security of the nuclear deterrent mission. The Alliance is committed to ensuring greater integration and coherence of capabilities and activities across all domains and the spectrum of conflict, while reaffirming the unique and distinct role of nuclear deterrence. NATO will continue to maintain credible deterrence, strengthen its strategic communications, enhance the effectiveness of its exercises and reduce strategic risks."

Nuclear Consultation

The key principles of NATO's nuclear policy are established by the Heads of State and Government of the 30 members of the Alliance. The development and implementation of NATO's nuclear policy are the responsibility of the Nuclear Planning Group (NPG). The NPG provides the forum for consultation on all issues that relate to NATO nuclear deterrence. All Allies, with the exception of France, which has decided not to participate, are members of the NPG.

The Role of NATO's Nuclear Forces

The fundamental purpose of NATO's nuclear forces is for deterrence. Nuclear weapons are unique and the circumstances under which NATO might have to use nuclear weapons are extremely remote. Furthermore, any employment of nuclear weapons against NATO would fundamentally alter the nature of a conflict. Should the fundamental security of any NATO Ally be threatened, NATO has the capabilities and the resolve to impose costs on the adversary that would be unacceptable and far outweigh the benefits that any adversary could hope to achieve.

Strategic Nuclear Forces

The strategic forces of the Alliance, and particularly those of the United States, are the supreme guarantee of the security of the Alliance. The independent strategic nuclear forces of the United

THE LEGALITY OF NUCLEAR WEAPONS

Nuclear weapons, together with biological and chemical weapons, are all categorized as weapons of mass destruction (as opposed to conventional weapons).

The term "nuclear weapons" is generally applied to the atomic bomb (A-bomb, whose effect depends on the rapid fission of the uranium or plutonium atom), the hydrogen or thermonuclear bomb (H-bomb, which uses the energy released by the fission of hydrogen isotopes at a very high temperature) and the neutron bomb (N-bomb, which causes minor material damage than the other two bombs, but whose radiation effects are more lethal).

There is no comprehensive prohibition of nuclear weapons, but only partial prohibitions, as follows:

- the prohibition to test, use, manufacture, produce, acquire, receive, stockpile, install, locate and possess nuclear weapons in a stated region
- Latin America: Treaty for the Prohibition of Nuclear Weapons in Latin America (Treaty of Tlatelolco), Mexico, 14 February 1967
- Africa: African Nuclear-Weapon-Free Zone Treaty (Treaty of Pelindaba), South Africa, 2 June 1995
- the prohibition to place nuclear weapons and other weapons of mass destruction on the bottom of the seas and oceans and in their subsoil
- Treaty on the Prohibition of the Emplacement of Nuclear Weapons and Other Weapons of Mass Destruction on the Sea-Bed and the Ocean Floor and in the Subsoil thereof, London, Moscow and Washington, 10 April 1971

Kingdom and France have a deterrent role of their own and contribute significantly to the overall security of the Alliance. These Allies' separate centres of decision-making contribute to deterrence by complicating the calculations of any potential adversaries. In other words, should an adversary decide to attack NATO, they must not only contend with NATO's decision-making, but also make a judgment about decision-making from the leaders of the United States, United Kingdom, and France.

- the prohibition to place in orbit around the earth and other celestial bodies devices carrying nuclear weapons or to place them on the surface or in the subsoil of the moon or other celestial bodies
- Treaty on Principles Governing the Activities of States in the Exploration and Use of Outer Space, including the Moon and Other Celestial Bodies, London, Moscow and Washington, 27 January 1967
- Agreement Governing the Activities of States on the Moon and Other Celestial Bodies, UN General Assembly, Resolution 34/68, 5 December 1979

On 8 July 1996, the International Court of Justice issued an Advisory Opinion concerning the legality of nuclear weapons. The Court noted the absence of a conventional prohibition on the use of nuclear weapons, but opined that the use of nuclear weapons must comply with the rules and principles of IHL, including the principle of distinction, proportionality and the prohibition of superfluous injury and unnecessary suffering. The ICJ has faced criticism for its ambiguous conclusions that "the threat or use of nuclear weapons would generally be contrary to the rules and principles of international law applicable in armed conflict, and in particular the principles of international humanitarian law," while at the same time claiming that it could not "conclude definitively whether the threat of use of nuclear weapons would be lawful or unlawful in an extreme circumstance of self-defence, in which the very survival of a State would be at stake."

"Nuclear Weapons," International Committee of the Red Cross (ICRC).

Dual-Capable Aircraft

NATO's nuclear deterrence posture also relies on the United States' nuclear weapons forward-deployed in Europe, as well as on the capabilities and infrastructure provided by Allies concerned. A number of NATO member countries contribute a dual-capable aircraft (DCA) capability to the Alliance. These aircraft are central to NATO's nuclear deterrence mission and are available for nuclear roles at various levels of readiness. In their nuclear role, the aircraft are equipped to carry nuclear bombs in a conflict and personnel are trained accordingly.

The United States maintains absolute control and custody of their nuclear weapons forward deployed in Europe, while Allies provide military support for the DCA mission with conventional forces and capabilities. Nuclear sharing arrangements play a vital role in the interconnection of the Alliance and remain one of the main components of security guarantees and the indivisibility of security of the whole Euro-Atlantic area.

Evolution of NATO's Nuclear Policy

Nuclear deterrence has been at the core of NATO's mutual security guarantee and collective defence since its inception in 1949. The very first NATO Strategic Concept (1949) referenced the requirement to "ensure the ability to carry out strategic bombing promptly by all means possible with all types of weapons without exception." The United States subsequently committed nuclear weapons to NATO in July 1953, with the first American theatre nuclear weapons arriving in Europe in September 1954. NATO's nuclear sharing arrangements, which were already in place by the time negotiations for the Nuclear Non-Proliferation Treaty (NPT) began in the 1960s, were codified by the United States and the Soviet Union as a precursor for the final agreed NPT text. The United Kingdom has also assigned its nuclear forces, including its current single submarine-based system and Continuous At-Sea Deterrent, to the protection of NATO Allies since 1962.

NATO seeks its security at the lowest possible level of forces and is fully committed to arms control, disarmament and non-proliferation. Since the height of the Cold War, it has reduced the size of its land-based nuclear weapons stockpile by over 90 per cent, reducing the number of nuclear weapons stationed in Europe and its reliance on nuclear weapons in strategy.

In response to Russia's unprovoked and unlawful war against Ukraine, at the extraordinary Summit on 24 March 2022, NATO Heads of State and Government affirmed that NATO will significantly strengthen its longer-term deterrence and defence posture and develop the full range of ready forces and capabilities necessary to maintain credible deterrence and defence. They further committed to enhancing preparedness and readiness for chemical, biological, radiological and nuclear threats. These decisions were reflected in the 2022 NATO Strategic Concept, which was adopted in June at the Madrid Summit.

Periodical and Internet Sources Bibliography

The following articles have been selected to supplement the diverse views presented in this chapter.

Julian Borger, "U.S. Will Soon Need to Deter Two Major Nuclear Powers for the First Time, White House Says," *Guardian*, October 12, 2022. https://www.theguardian.com/world/2022/oct/12/nuclear-weapons-russia-china-us-national-security-strategy.

Matthew R. Costlow, "The U.S. Needs More Nuclear Weapons," *Wall Street Journal*, January 30, 2022. https://www.wsj.com/articles/the-us-needs-more-nuclear-weapons-global-powers-china-russia-defense-modernization-11643567183.

Elisabeth Eaves, "Why Is America Getting a New $100 Billion Nuclear Weapon?" Bulletin of the Atomic Scientists, February 8, 2021. https://thebulletin.org/2021/02/why-is-america-getting-a-new-100-billion-nuclear-weapon/.

William Hartung, "Why Are We Still Building Nuclear Weapons? Follow the Money," *Forbes*, August 10, 2021. https://www.forbes.com/sites/williamhartung/2021/08/10/why-are-we-still-building-nuclear-weapons----follow-the-money/?sh=1917f9958887.

Yint Hmu, "A New Nuclear Weapons Delivery System Is the Last Thing the U.S. Needs," *Hill*, November 21, 2022. https://thehill.com/opinion/national-security/3745138-a-new-nuclear-weapons-delivery-system-is-the-last-thing-the-us-needs/.

Matthew Kendrick, "U.S. Allies Trust the American Nuclear Umbrella, Even If They Hate Nuclear Weapons," Morning Consult, August 30, 2022. https://morningconsult.com/2022/08/30/united-states-allies-nuclear-weapons-umbrella-trust-survey/.

Adam Lowther, "3 Reasons Why America's Massive Nuclear Arsenal Actually Makes the World Safer," *Business Insider*, July 21, 2017. https://www.businessinsider.com/3-reasons-why-americas-massive-nuclear-arsenal-actually-makes-the-world-safer-2017-7.

Dan Plesch, "Could the U.S. Win World War III Without Using Nuclear Weapons?" Conversation, April 19, 2018. https://theconversation.com/could-the-us-win-world-war-iii-without-using-nuclear-weapons-94771.

R. Jeffrey Smith, "The U.S. Nuclear Arsenal Is Becoming More Destructive and Possibly More Risky," The Center for Public Integrity, October 29, 2021. https://publicintegrity.org/national-security/future-of-warfare/nuclear-weapon-arsenal-more-destructive-risky/.

Stephen M. Walt, "It's Time to Fold America's Nuclear Umbrella," *Foreign Policy,* March 23, 2021. https://foreignpolicy.com/2021/03/23/its-time-to-fold-americas-nuclear-umbrella/.

OPPOSING
VIEWPOINTS®
SERIES

CHAPTER 3

Is Nuclear Disarmament Possible?

Chapter Preface

W hile the global nuclear arsenal has shrunken considerably since its peak during the Cold War, complete nuclear disarmament has proven difficult. This is commonly attributed to geopolitical tension between the U.S. and its allies and their potential adversaries, which include Russia, China, North Korea, and Iran.[1] Mutual suspicion encourages these nuclear weapon states (NWSs) to maintain a nuclear stockpile in order to deter an attack from adversaries and to ensure they can defend themselves and their allies in the event of an attack.

However, a nuclear attack would cause a massive number of civilian deaths both during the attack and in its aftermath, making the potential use of nuclear weapons a humanitarian crisis. As a result, the UN, the governments of numerous individual countries (primarily non-nuclear weapon states), civilians, and humanitarian organizations have urged NWSs to embrace nuclear disarmament for the safety of all humankind.

Since nuclear weapons were first created, there have been multiple treaties created to promote nuclear disarmament and nonproliferation. A landmark international treaty is the Treaty on the Non-Proliferation of Nuclear Weapons, commonly known as the Non-Proliferation Treaty (NPT). The treaty was created by a UN-sponsored organization and was signed into force in 1970.[2] Though one of the treaty's goals is to promote nuclear disarmament, its main goal is to prevent the spread of nuclear weapons, also known as nuclear proliferation. However, decades later in 2021, the Treaty on the Prohibition of Nuclear Weapons (TPNW)—another UN treaty—entered into force.[3] This treaty prohibits nuclear weapons for all countries that are party to it. Unfortunately, though, no NWS has supported or signed the treaty, limiting its effectiveness.

But this doesn't mean the fight for nuclear arms control is futile. NWSs have created their own treaties to limit the development and use of nuclear weapons. Since the Cold War, the U.S. has entered into numerous nuclear agreements with Russia (and formerly the USSR). The most recent treaty is the New Strategic Arms Reduction Treaty (New START), which was signed in 2010 and is considered a legally binding agreement that limits the number of nuclear warheads and related infrastructure each country can possess.[4] The agreement was extended to 2026, but in February 2023 Russia suspended its participation due to the war in Ukraine.[5]

The Joint Comprehensive Plan of Action (JCPOA) agreement between Iran and China, France, Russia, United Kingdom, United States, Germany, and European Union (EU) is another agreement between countries that was intended to limit nuclear weapons. The agreement was made in 2015 and stipulated that Iran would largely dismantle its nuclear program and allow inspections of its nuclear facilities in exchange for sanctions' relief from other countries.[6] However, although Iran initially complied with the deal, former President Trump withdrew from the deal in 2018, and shortly after that Iran resumed building its nuclear program in defiance of the agreement.[7]

Many challenges stand in the way of nuclear disarmament, but it has the support of civilians, national governments, and nongovernmental organizations around the world, and some argue that it is essential for the security of humanity. This chapter considers the arguments for disarmament, the history of this process, and the challenges that make disarmament difficult, along with potential solutions.

Notes

1. Hans Kristensen and Matt Korda, "The 2022 Nuclear Posture Review: Arms Control Subdued by Military Rivalry," Federation of American Scientists, October 27, 2022. https://fas.org/blogs/security/2022/10/2022-nuclear-posture-review/.
2. "Treaty on the Non-Proliferation of Nuclear Weapons (NPT)," United Nation Office for Disarmament Affairs. https://www.un.org/disarmament/wmd/nuclear/npt/.
3. "Treaty on the Prohibition of Nuclear Weapons," United Nations Office for Disarmament Affairs. https://www.un.org/disarmament/wmd/nuclear/tpnw/.
4. Daryl Kimball, "U.S.-Russian Nuclear Arms Control Agreements at a Glance," Arms Control Association, October 2022. https://www.armscontrol.org/factsheets/USRussiaNuclearAgreements.

5. Agence France Presse, "Putin Says Moscow Suspending Participation in New START Nuclear Treaty," *Barron's,* February 21, 2023. https://www.barrons.com/news/putin-says-moscow-suspending-participation-in-new-start-nuclear-treaty-d307fa0f.

6. Kali Robinson, "What Is the Iran Nuclear Deal?" Council on Foreign Relations, July 20, 2022. https://www.cfr.org/backgrounder/what-iran-nuclear-deal.

7. *Ibid.*

"Certain national governments and members of civil society have cooperated on initiatives to promote progress towards a world free of nuclear weapons."

Many Efforts Are Being Made to Promote Nuclear Disarmament

Nuclear Threat Initiative

In this excerpted viewpoint from the Nuclear Threat Initiative (NTI), the organization explains the various efforts that have been made to promote nuclear disarmament. Bilateral efforts for nuclear arms control have been made by the U.S. and Russia (formerly the USSR). Agreements between the two countries have placed limitations on their nuclear arsenals since the Cold War. However, recent tensions between the U.S. and Russia threaten the progress that has been made. Multilateral nuclear weapons treaties— meaning those involving more than two countries—have also been challenging to put into effect despite efforts from the UN. This is largely because of lack of cooperation from the U.S. and Russia. However, national governments, members of civil society, and humanitarian groups have helped make progress in disarmament. The Nuclear Threat Initiative is a nonprofit, nonpartisan global security organization focused on reducing nuclear and biological threats imperiling humanity.

"Overview of the Nuclear Disarmament Resource Collection," Nuclear Threat Initiative (NTI), October 20, 2021. Reprinted by permission. Produced by the James Martin Center for Nonproliferation Studies for the Nuclear Threat Initiative, www.nti.org.

As you read, consider the following questions:

1. According to this viewpoint, when did the U.S. and Russia/the USSR start limiting their nuclear arsenals?
2. At the time this viewpoint was published, how many countries had not ratified the Comprehensive Nuclear Test-Ban Treaty (CTBT)?
3. Which former high-ranking U.S. officials took a stand against nuclear weapons in a 2007 *Wall Street Journal* op-ed?

[…]

Gauging progress towards nuclear disarmament is complicated because shifts in numbers of weapons and the overarching policies governing these weapons are relevant. In terms of quantitative reductions, measurable steps have been undertaken by key nuclear weapon states (NWS) both unilaterally and bilaterally. The NWS collectively reduced the size of their nuclear arsenals from over 70,000 warheads at the height of the Cold War to approximately 14,200 by 2018. [1] These reductions have been carried out unilaterally by at least four NWS, as well as through bilateral legally binding arrangements between the United States and the Soviet Union/Russian Federation.

The United States has reduced its stockpile by about 87% from a Cold War peak of 31,255 warheads in 1967, to the current stockpile of approximately 4,000 operational and reserved warheads. [2] While France has reduced its arsenal unilaterally, and the United Kingdom announced ambitious reductions to its arsenal in 2010, both states plan to maintain a credible nuclear deterrent for the foreseeable future. [3] China is the only NWS that appears to be increasing its nuclear stockpile, albeit slowly. [4] Experts estimate that India and Pakistan have been rapidly expanding their nuclear arsenals and capabilities.[5]

Bilateral Efforts

There is an extensive precedent for bilateral U.S.-USSR/ Russia arms control. Since 1969, the United States and Russia have been limiting/reducing their strategic nuclear arsenals limiting the number of ICBMs and SLBMs, leaving both nations to increase numbers of both bombers and warheads. SALT I also produced the ABM treaty in 1972, which banned nationwide strategic missile defenses (the U.S. withdrew from the ABM treaty in 2002). [6] Following the Cold War, START I (enacted in 1994), placed limitations on the numbers of deployed launchers and, for the first time, warheads. While both START II and III failed to materialize, the United States and Russia negotiated the Strategic Offensive Reductions Treaty (SORT) in 2002. SORT provided for a significant reduction of deployed strategic nuclear warheads in each arsenal to 1,700—2,200. However, SORT was often criticized for having a weak verification regime that relied on the START I regime. Fears that this treaty and the START agreement would expire without anything to fill the void were allayed with the signing of the New START Treaty in April 2010, and its subsequent entry into force in February 2011. New START limits the United States and Russia to no more than 1,550 deployed nuclear warheads and 700 launchers by 2018. [7] Both the United States and Russia met those limits on schedule, according to a February 2018 information exchange. [8]

New START expires in 2021, and tensions between the U.S. and Russia complicate negotiations for further strategic reductions. [9] Both countries are pursuing new types of weapons: at a speech in March 2018, Russian President Vladimir Putin announced several new nuclear weapon delivery systems, including an intercontinental cruise missile, while U.S. President Donald Trump's 2018 Nuclear Posture Review called for lower-yield warheads for submarine-launched ballistic missiles and submarine-launched cruise missiles. [10]

Multilateral Efforts

Attempts at negotiating legally binding multilateral nuclear disarmament treaties have proven challenging. The United Nations established the Conference on Disarmament (CD) as the sole multilateral disarmament-negotiating forum in 1979. The 65-member, consensus-ruled body has only negotiated one treaty related to nuclear disarmament over the past 30 years, the Comprehensive Nuclear Test-Ban Treaty (CTBT) in 1996. Widely considered to be a milestone towards nuclear disarmament, the CTBT would prohibit all nuclear testing. Nineteen years after it opened for signature the CTBT has yet to enter into force. Entry into force of the CTBT requires ratification by all states with nuclear power reactors and/or research reactors (in 1996), known as Annex II states. Eight of these countries, including the United States and China, have yet to ratify. [11]

Since the conclusion of CTBT negotiations in 1996, the CD has been locked in a perpetual stalemate. Negotiations on a Fissile Material Cut-Off Treaty (FMCT) have not commenced even 18 years after agreement on the Shannon Mandate (a mandate adopted by the CD in 1995 that proposed the negotiation of a treaty banning the production of fissile material [12]). Many consider an FMCT ripe for negotiation and the next logical step toward nuclear disarmament. In 2009, CD member states agreed upon a program of work, CD/1864, but were unable to implement it due to procedural blockages. [13] Over the past three years Pakistan has emerged as the single detractor, objecting on the basis of national security and substance. Pakistan fears its national security will be at risk if its rival and neighbor, India, is left with a larger existing fissile material stockpile, and therefore has the capability to continue to produce nuclear weapons after the implementation of the treaty. [14] Pakistan argues that an FMCT would not address existing stockpiles of fissile materials, and would therefore further nonproliferation but not disarmament. [15]

Pakistan's conceptual argument taps into the longstanding confrontation between the nuclear weapon "haves and have nots." Paradoxically, as Non-Aligned Movement (NAM) members, Pakistan and India vocally support nuclear disarmament while simultaneously increasing their nuclear arsenals and delivery systems. Many NAM members and other non-nuclear weapon states (NNWS) believe that the NWS are not fully meeting their Article VI obligation. [16] Apart from the bilateral negotiations on New START, there have been no negotiations or efforts on disarmament measures since the conclusion of the CTBT negotiations. Moreover, unilateral and U.S.-Russia reductions have been perceived by many NNWS as nothing more than efforts to streamline existing nuclear arsenals, rather than steps towards complete nuclear disarmament. Perhaps most notably, all nuclear weapon states are pursuing some degree of nuclear modernization. [17]

Other Significant Efforts to Promote Nuclear Disarmament

Certain national governments and members of civil society have cooperated on initiatives to promote progress towards a world free of nuclear weapons. A progressive approach to promote nuclear disarmament was taken by the New Agenda Coalition (NAC). In June 1998, foreign ministers from Brazil, Egypt, Ireland, Mexico, New Zealand, South Africa, Slovenia, and Sweden (the latter two eventually withdrawing), issued a statement calling for a new nuclear disarmament agenda, "Toward a Nuclear-Weapons-Free World: Time for a New Agenda." The NAC played an instrumental role in convincing the NWS to agree to the thirteen practical steps towards nuclear disarmament in the final document of the 2000 NPT Review Conference.

Around the same time, the Middle Powers Initiative was established to support NNWS efforts to reduce and eliminate worldwide nuclear weapons arsenals. Following the failure of the 2005 NPT Review Conference, the Middle Powers Initiative launched the "Article VI Forum" in October 2005 to examine the legal, technical, and political requirements to fulfill nonproliferation and disarmament commitments for a nuclear weapon-free world. [18]

Several independent international commissions have played an important role by providing expert recommendations in the form of nuclear disarmament action plans. These commissions include the 1996 Canberra Commission on the Elimination of Nuclear Weapons sponsored by the Australian government, the 1998 Tokyo Forum for Nuclear Nonproliferation and Disarmament sponsored by the Japanese government, and the Weapons of Mass Destruction (WMD) Commission.

The Weapons of Mass Destruction Commission was established in 2003 amidst stagnation on nuclear disarmament and serious challenges facing the nuclear nonproliferation regime. It issued a report that concluded "the nuclear weapon states no longer seem to take their commitment to nuclear disarmament seriously-even though this was an essential part of the NPT bargain, both at the treaty's birth in 1968 and when it was extended indefinitely in 1995." [19] The report offered several recommendations for multilateral cooperative actions to counter this trend, including a call to adhere to disarmament obligations, ratify the CTBT and FMCT, and change nuclear postures.

An initiative undertaken by four former high-ranking U.S. officials—George Shultz, William Perry, Henry Kissinger, and Sam Nunn—created significant momentum for a world free of nuclear weapons. The four statesmen originally published their proposals in a 4 January 2007 *Wall Street Journal* op-ed, "A World Free of Nuclear Weapons," followed a year later by another op-ed, "Toward a Nuclear Weapon Free World." This initiative came at a critical juncture, with the international community facing new and ongoing nuclear threats, when no new significant arms control reductions between the United States and Russia were being pursued. [20] The four statesmen called for U.S. leadership and global cooperation on nonproliferation.

In 2008, Japan and Australia established the International Commission on Nuclear Non-Proliferation and Disarmament

(ICNND) to reinvigorate international nonproliferation and disarmament efforts and to help shape a consensus at the then-upcoming 2010 NPT Review Conference. Japan and Australia joined together again in September 2010 to create the Nonproliferation and Disarmament Initiative (NPDI). The group consisted of twelve countries (Australia, Canada, Chile, Germany, Japan, Mexico, the Netherlands, Nigeria, the Philippines, Poland, Turkey and the United Arab Emirates) that aimed to facilitate the implementation of the measures from the consensus document of the 2010 NPT Review Conference. [21] In April 2014, the NPDI adopted the "Hiroshima Declaration" that contained concrete proposals for both disarmament and nonproliferation, including calls to negotiate the FMCT, increase nuclear safety and safeguards, encourage the entry into force of the CTBT, and increase transparency in disarmament reporting. [22] However, as the NPDI consists mainly of U.S. allies protected by U.S. extended nuclear deterrence, its disarmament approach is often considered more moderate than the ones of the NAC or NAM that call for delegitimizing nuclear weapons.

The Humanitarian Initiative for Nuclear Disarmament

The humanitarian impact of nuclear weapons has increasingly drawn attention. The 2010 NPT Review Conference final document expressed concern about the humanitarian consequences of any use of nuclear weapons. [23] A coalition of state parties and civil society groups continued to push this issue, resulting in three international conferences on the humanitarian impact of nuclear weapons in Oslo, Nayarit, and Vienna, where discussions about negotiating a prohibition against nuclear weapons were held. [24] The third conference in Vienna produced the Humanitarian Pledge (formerly the "Austrian Pledge"), which over 100 countries have supported. [25]The statement emphasized that nuclear weapons should never be used again "under any circumstances." [26] The nuclear weapon states did not participate in the first two conferences, but the United States and United Kingdom sent representatives to attend the third conference in Vienna. [27] Another group of state parties, mainly consisting of NNWS who rely on U.S. extended nuclear deterrence has pushed an alternative humanitarian pledge that is less extensive. [28]

In response to the humanitarian initiative, the five NPT-recognized NWS initiated the so-called "P5 step," affirming that they intend to continue seeking progress on the step-by-step approach to nuclear disarmament as opposed to aiming to eliminate nuclear weapons within a specific timeframe. [29] The P-5 states have held seven conferences to increase dialogue and transparency in disarmament progress. For that purpose, at the 2015 Review Conference, each of the P5 states submitted its national report and completed a first edition of a glossary of key nuclear terms. However, most of the NNWS, especially NAM countries and civil society members, are critical about the P5 process since it is generally perceived that this process has not contributed to the actual reduction of nuclear weapons. [30]

Since the CD remains stalemated and the five NPT-recognized NWS have continually refused to participate in other multilateral negotiations on nuclear disarmament, the international community's ability to advance nuclear disarmament is highly limited. [31]

The important role of disarmament and nonproliferation education in promoting and facilitating nuclear disarmament must also be recognized, as evinced by the adoption of UN General Assembly Resolution 57/60 in November 2002, which reaffirms the need to support education in the field and include the topic in future meetings. [32] Education and training will remain vital to the success of future disarmament initiatives.

Nuclear Weapons Ban Treaty

After the failure of states parties to the 2015 NPT Review Conference to reach consensus, many countries sought to press forward the nuclear disarmament agenda in the United Nations

General Assembly. Over the course of three sessions in 2016, an Open-Ended Working Group (OEWG) of states recommended that the UN General Assembly convene a conference in 2017 to "negotiate a legally binding instrument to prohibit nuclear weapons, leading toward their total elimination." [33] On 27 October 2016, The First Committee of the UN General Assembly voted to adopt the resolution to convene the nuclear ban conference, and the full UN General Assembly followed suit on 23 December 2016. [34]

On 7 July 2017, the Treaty on the Prohibition of Nuclear Weapons was adopted by a recorded vote of 122 in favor to one against (the Netherlands), with one abstention (Singapore). [35] Proponents of the treaty believe that it can strengthen norms against nuclear weapons and stigmatize such weapons. Opponents, including nuclear possessing states and states under extended nuclear deterrence, boycotted the negotiations (with the exception of the Netherlands). NWS are sharply critical of the treaty process; France, the UK, and the U.S. assert that the treaty deepens the division between nuclear weapon states and non-nuclear weapon states, and jointly stated that they do not "intend to sign, ratify or ever become party to it." [36] Russia used similar language, claiming the treaty would "have a destabilizing effect on the nonproliferation regime." [37] However, the majority of the international community welcomed the adoption of the treaty as a significant achievement. In recognition of civil society's role and grass-roots activism in the treaty's passage, the International Campaign to Abolish Nuclear Weapons (ICAN) was awarded the 2017 Nobel Peace Prize for its "ground-breaking efforts to achieve a treaty-based prohibition of nuclear weapons." [38] As part of an effort to build bridges between parties with opposing views, the Japanese government established the "Group of Eminent Persons for Substantive Advancement of Nuclear Disarmament," and submitted its recommendations to the second session of the PrepCom for the 2020 NPT Review Conference. [39] On 24 October 2020, Honduras became the 50th state to ratify the Treaty on the Prohibition of Nuclear Weapons, meeting the threshold for the treaty's entry into force 90 days later on 22 January 2021. [40]

Notes

1. "Status of World Nuclear Forces," Federation of American Scientists, March 2018, https://fas.org.

2. Fact Sheet Increasing Transparency in the U.S. Nuclear Weapons Stockpile, U.S. Department of Defense, www.defense.gov; Hans M. Kristensen and Robert S. Norris, "US Nuclear Forces, 2018," Bulletin of the Atomic Scientists, Volume 74 (2), 4 March 2018, www.thebulletin.org.

3. "Securing Britain in an Age of Uncertainty: The Strategic Defence and Security Review," Prime Minister of the United Kingdom by Command of Her Majesty (London: Crown Copyright, 2010); "The French White Paper on Defence and National Security," Presidency of the Republic of France, 5 December 2008, www.cfr.org.

4. Shannon N. Kile and Hans M Kristensen, "Trends in World Nuclear Forces, 2017," SIPRI, July 2017, www.sipri.org.

5. Shannon N. Kile and Hans M Kristensen, "Trends in World Nuclear Forces, 2017," SIPRI, July 2017, www.sipri.org.

6. "U.S.-Soviet/Russian Nuclear Arms Control," *Arms Control Today* 32 (June 2002), www.armscontrol.org; Daryl Kimball and Tom Collina, "The Anti-Ballistic Missile Treaty at a Glance," Arms Control Association, updated January 2003, www.armscontrol.org.

7. Amy F. Woolf, "The New START Treaty: Central Limits and Key Provisions," Congressional Research Service, 18 June 2010, www.crs.gov.

8. U.S. Department of State, "New START Treaty Aggregate Numbers of Strategic Offensive Arms," Bureau of Arms Control, Verification and Compliance, 22 February 2018, www.state.gov.

9. Nikolai Sokov, "New START Expires in 3 Years. And Nobody Knows What Comes Next," *The National Interest,* 6 February 2018, www.nationalinterest.org.

10. Vladimir Putin, "Presidential Address to the Federal Assembly," 1 March 2018, https://en.kremlin.ru. Office of the Secretary of Defense, "Nuclear Posture Review, 2018," pp.54-55, www.defense.gov.

11. The other six states that have yet to ratify the CTBT include the DPRK, India, Pakistan, Egypt, Iran and Israel. The latest to ratify was Indonesia in February 2012. "Status of Signature and Ratification: Annex II States Only," Preparatory Commission for the Comprehensive Nuclear-Test-Ban Treaty Organization, updated February 2012, www.ctbto.org.

12. Paul Meyer, "Is There Any Fizz Left in the Fissban? Prospects for a Fissile Material Cutoff Treaty," *Arms Control Today,* December 2007, www.armscontrol.org.

13. Ray Acheson, "The Conference on Disarmament in 2009: Could do Better," *Disarmament Diplomacy* 91 (Summer 2009), www.acronym.org.uk.

14. Paul Meyer, "Free the Fissile Material Cut-Off Treaty: Functionality over Forum," *Bulletin of the Atomic Scientists: Web Edition*, 19 September 2011, www.thebulletin.org; A.H Nayyar and Zia Mian, "Pakistan," in the publication Reducing and Eliminating Nuclear Weapons: Country Perspectives on the Challenges to Nuclear Disarmament, International Panel on Fissile Materials, May 2010, www.fissilematerials.org.

15. The Shannon Mandate, as contained in CD/1299, was agreed upon in March 1995 as the basis for negotiations of a FMCT. Document text, www.reachingcriticalwill.org.

16. John Burroughs, "Reaching Nuclear Disarmament," *Beyond Arms Control: Challenges and choices for nuclear disarmament,* ed. Ray Acheson (New York: Reaching Critical Will, 2010), pp. 161-162.

17. Ray Acheson, "Introduction" in the publication *Assuring Destruction Forever,* Reaching Critical Will, March 2012, www.reachingcriticalwill.org.

18. "About MPI," Middle Powers Initiative, 8 August 2011, www.middlepowers.org.

19. Hans Blix, "Weapons of Terror: Freeing the World of Nuclear, Biological, and Chemical Arms," Weapons of Mass Destruction Commission (Stockholm), 1 June 2006, www.wmdcommission.org.

20. "Toward a World Free of Nuclear Weapons," *Wall Street Journal Op-Ed,* George P Shultz, William J. Perry, Henry A. Kissinger and Sam Nunn, 15 January 2008; "A World Free of Nuclear Weapons" *Wall Street Journal* Op-Ed, George P Shultz, William J. Perry, Henry A. Kissinger and Sam Nunn, 4 January 2007.

21. Tom Bayur of Turkey on behalf of the Nonproliferation and Disarmament Initiative (NPDI), The NPDI Joint Statement to the NPT PrepCom, 30 April 2012, www.reachingcriticalwill.org.

22. Department of Foreign Affairs and Trade, "Non-Proliferation and Disarmament Initiative," Australian Government, www.dfat.gov.au.

23. 2010 NPT Review Conference Final Document, NPT/CONF.2010/50 (Vol. I), May 2010, www.un.org.

24. Report and Summary of Findings of the Conference, Vienna Conference on the Humanitarian Impact of Nuclear Weapons, 8-9 December 2015, www.reachingcriticalwill.org.

25. Joint Statement on the P5 Beijing Conference: Enhancing Strategic Confidence and Working Together to Implement the Nuclear Non-Proliferation Review Outcomes, US Department of State, 15 April 2014, www.state.gov.

26. Sebastian Kurz, Joint Statement on Behalf of the Humanitarian Impact of Nuclear Weapons at the 2015 NPT Review Conference, 28 April 2015, www.reachingcriticalwill.org.

27. Ray Acheson, "Filling the gap: report from the Vienna conference on the humanitarian impact of nuclear weapons," *Reaching Critical Will,* December 2014, www.reachingcriticalwill.org.

28. Statement by H.E Gillian Bird, Ambassador and Permanent Member of Australia to the United Nations at the 2015 NPT Review Conference, 30 April 2015, www.reachingcriticalwill.org.

29. Joint Statement on the P5 Beijing Conference: Enhancing Strategic Confidence and Working Together to Implement the Nuclear Non-Proliferation Review Outcomes, US Department of State, 15 April 2014, www.state.gov.

30. Statement by the People's Republic of China, France, the Russian Federation, the United Kingdom of Great Britain and Northern Ireland, and the United States of America to the 2015 Treaty on the Non-Proliferation of Nuclear Weapons Review Conference, 30 April 2015, www.reachingcriticalwill.org.

31. Ray Acheson, "NWS labelled 'persistent underachievers' in the NPT yearbook," *Reaching Critical Will,* 26 April 2013, www.reachingcriticalwill.org.

32. "United Nations Study on Disarmament and Non-Proliferation Education," United Nations General Assembly Resolution A/RES/57/60, 30 December 2002, www.un.org.

33. "Taking Forward Multilateral Nuclear Disarmament Negotiations," United Nations General Assembly Agenda Item A/C.1/71/L.41, 14 October 2016, www.un.org.
34. "Taking Forward Multilateral Nuclear Disarmament Negotiations," United Nations General Assembly Resolution A/RES/71/258, 23 December 2017, www.un.org.
35. United Nations Press Release, "United Nations Conference to Negotiate Ban on Nuclear Weapons Holds First Organizational Meeting, Adopts Agenda for 2017 Substantive Session," 23 February 2017, www.un.org.
36. UN News, "UN Conference Adopts Treaty Banning Nuclear Weapons," www.un.org.
37. Joint Press Statement from the Permanent Representatives to the United Nations of the United States, United Kingdom, and France Following the Adoption of a Treaty Banning Nuclear Weapons, 7 July 2017, https://usun.state.gov.
38. "Russia Doesn't Plan to Join Treaty on Prohibition of Nuclear Weapons – Lavrov," *Sputnik News*, 19 January 2018, www.sputniknews.com.
39. "Group of Eminent Persons for Substantive Advancement of Nuclear Disarmament," Japanese Ministry of Foreign Affairs Website, www.mofa.go.jp.
40. The treaty stipulates that the first meeting of states parties will convene within one year of the treaty's entry into force. "Historic milestone: UN Treaty on the Prohibition of Nuclear Weapons reaches 50 ratifications needed for entry into force," ICAN news update, accessed 15 December 2020, www.icanw.org.

> "Despite repeated and sometimes intense efforts to put disarmament efforts on track, the United Nations was unable to devise negotiating schemes that would bring the different parties together."

Nuclear Disarmament Will Not Be Possible if Nuclear Weapon States Resist It

Miguel Marín-Bosch

In this viewpoint, Miguel Marín-Bosch examines the history of nuclear weapons and attempts at disarmament. Although it is widely acknowledged that nuclear weapons pose an existential threat to all of humankind, attempts to get countries to agree on disarmament have been difficult. Countries that possess nuclear weapons are reluctant to give up their arsenals because of suspicion toward their rivals. The volatile relationship between the U.S. and Russia also poses a challenge to disarmament. While former President Obama was in support of nuclear disarmament, increased tension between the countries in recent years has made this seem increasingly unlikely. Miguel Marín-Bosch was formerly Mexico's ambassador to the Conference on Disarmament and chaired the first year of the Comprehensive Nuclear Test Ban Treaty negotiations.

From "A Nuclear-Weapons-Free World: Is It Achievable?" by Miguel Marín-Bosch. Copyright © 2022 United Nations. Used with the permission of the United Nations.

As you read, consider the following questions:

1. According to this viewpoint, why doesn't the UN Charter mention nuclear weapons?
2. What does Marín-Bosch consider to be the drawbacks of the Baruch Plan?
3. According to this viewpoint, what are some of the challenges former President Barack Obama faced in his efforts for nuclear disarmament?

After the worst of times, we are perhaps entering the best of times for proponents of nuclear disarmament. At long last, advocates of the elimination of nuclear weapons have reason for some guarded optimism. The road to a nuclear-weapons-free world will be long and bumpy, but those expected to take the initiative seem to have finally decided to lead. That is encouraging.

Sixty-four years ago the world was free of nuclear weapons, but after the production of some 140,000 of these artifacts of mass destruction, there seems to be a significant shift in the role some Governments have assigned to them. They are no longer generally considered to be the best means to ensure national security. Deterrence and mutually-assured destruction have become outdated concepts in a world now more concerned with other questions and challenges, including widespread poverty, climate change, a worldwide economic and financial meltdown, and other threats such as the recent alarm over the pandemic outbreak of a new kind of influenza virus.

Above all, the motivation for seeking the elimination of nuclear weapons now seems to be a fear of the further proliferation of these weapons to other States and possibly to the so-called non-State actors, including terrorist groups. There is the rub.

Nuclear weapons are intrinsically dangerous and pose an unparalleled threat to the very existence of humankind. They do not enhance a country's security but, rather, imperil the survival of all nations, which should be the point of departure of nuclear disarmament efforts.

To dwell on the potential danger that they may fall into the wrong hands is to misconstrue the argument for their elimination. They should be banned because they are immoral—and probably illegal—tools of destruction. Since their use would likely be fatal for all, they cannot even be considered instruments of war.

The twin questions of nuclear weapons and nuclear energy have been on the agenda of the United Nations since its beginning: the dawn of the atomic age coincided with its birth. The UN Charter, however, makes no mention of nuclear weapons for the simple reason that it was adopted at the San Francisco conference three weeks before the first test and six weeks before their use in Hiroshima and Nagasaki. The transcendental nature of the discovery of atomic energy prompted the delegates to the UN General Assembly's first session to address the issue immediately. In its very first resolution—1 (I) of 24 January 1946—the Assembly established the Atomic Energy Commission, composed of the Security Council members and Canada, and requested that it submit specific proposals for ensuring the use of atomic energy for peaceful purposes only, for the elimination of atomic and other weapons of mass destruction and for the establishment of a system of safeguards, including inspections, to prevent violations and evasions.

A number of specific proposals followed, including one by the United States in June 1946. As the only nuclear-weapon State (NWS), it was natural that the United States put forward its own ideas on the matter. These were contained in what became known as the Baruch Plan, which was based largely on the United States government publication A Report on the International Control of Atomic Energy, issued in March of that year.

The U.S., which still held an unchallenged nuclear monopoly, called for an open exchange among all nations of basic scientific information for peaceful ends; control of atomic energy to the extent necessary to ensure its use only for peaceful purposes;

the elimination of atomic weapons and all other major weapons adaptable to mass destruction from national arsenals; and the establishment of effective safeguards by way of inspection and other means to protect complying States against the hazards of violations and evasions.

Though forward-thinking in many aspects, the Baruch Plan had several drawbacks. The most controversial one was probably its insistence that the United States retain its nuclear stockpile (which then consisted of nine weapons) until it was satisfied with the effectiveness of the international control system.[1] This proved unacceptable to the USSR, which wanted to reverse the order: all should first surrender their nuclear weapons and then implement an international verification system. One will never know if the world might have returned in 1946 to its nuclear-weapons-free status. What we do know is that there followed four decades of an unbridled nuclear arms race between the U.S. and the Union of Soviet Socialist Republics (USSR) and the acquisition of those weapons and their delivery systems by other nations.

After the USSR's first nuclear test in 1949, the United Kingdom followed in 1952, France in 1960, China in 1964, India in 1974 and Pakistan in 1998. Israel also acquired nuclear weapons as did South Africa, which later surrendered its stockpile. After the USSR's collapse, Belarus, Kazakhstan and Ukraine became for a time de facto NWS. The Democratic People's Republic of Korea has also tested a nuclear device. In addition, there are many countries that possess the scientific know-how, technology and fissile material that would allow them to play the nuclear card in a relatively short time.

In 1952 the U.S. achieved a qualitative leap in the nuclear-arms race when it detonated its first thermonuclear device. A year later the USSR followed suit.

The development of nuclear-weapons delivery systems—bombers, missiles and submarines—is another chapter of the arms race. However, the testing of nuclear weapons and the rockets to transport them would eventually rally public opinion (at least momentarily) in favour of nuclear disarmament measures.

Despite repeated and sometimes intense efforts to put disarmament efforts on track, the United Nations was unable to devise negotiating schemes that would bring the different parties together. Deep-rooted suspicion of the rival's motives and the absence of political will ensured a negotiating stalemate for almost two decades.

In the early 1960s the U.S. and the USSR finally agreed to lead disarmament talks at the Geneva Eighteen-Nation Disarmament Committee (endc) meeting. Calls for an end to nuclear tests, especially in the atmosphere, and a stop to further horizontal proliferation were instrumental in getting the endc going in 1962. Not surprisingly, the first order of business was a treaty to ban nuclear-weapons tests in the atmosphere, under water and in outer space. The 1963 Partial Test-Ban Treaty was agreed upon rather quickly. It did not contain verification measures and it prohibited activities which the endc's three participating nuclear-weapon States -- the UK, the U.S. and the USSR (France refused to take its seat at the table) -- were ready to forego. Underground testing would continue for over 30 years.

The next item on the endc's agenda was a multilateral legal agreement to prevent the further spread of nuclear weapons to other nations (horizontal proliferation). The 1968 Treaty on the Non-Proliferation of Nuclear Weapons (NPT) has become the cornerstone of nuclear disarmament efforts since its entry into force in 1970.

By the late 1950s, the possible spread of nuclear weapons to more countries (horizontal proliferation) had become a source of increasing concern. So had the continued improvement of existing arsenals (vertical proliferation) and the testing of those weapons was seen as the key element of the qualitative nuclear arms race. Both horizontal proliferation and nuclear testing had found their way onto the United Nations agenda.

By the mid-1960s a number of countries had decided to forego the nuclear option and agreed to a trade-off from the nuclear-weapon States in return for a legally-binding commitment to remain non-nuclear-weapon States (nNWS). It was time to sit down and negotiate a treaty. Countries in Latin America had already begun the pioneering efforts to establish a nuclear-weapon-free zone in their region, which they saw as a way to begin to achieve a nuclear-weapons-free world.

The NPT's approach was different. It rests on three pillars: horizontal non-proliferation; vertical non-proliferation and nuclear disarmament; and the peaceful uses of nuclear energy. It is a contract between NWS and nNWS. The latter would enjoy the benefits of the peaceful uses of nuclear energy and refrain from acquiring nuclear weapons. The former would pursue nuclear disarmament, beginning with the cessation of all nuclear tests.

By then, the International Atomic Energy Agency (IAEA) was in place, providing all parties with an international verification system, including inspections. The IAEA would do the same for the nuclear-weapon-free zones that have been established.

The NPT was done in good faith, but the non-nuclear-weapon States insisted that the situation regarding its implementation be reviewed periodically; thus the five-year conferences. In addition, the NPT was a temporary agreement whose extension would have to be examined after 25 years. In 1995 it was extended indefinitely.

After 1970, despite some very limited bilateral agreements between the U.S. and the USSR, the nuclear arms race continued. The 1963 Partial Test-Ban Treaty had been a hoax, since underground tests multiplied. It appeared that since nuclear tests were out of sight, they were also out of mind. Calls for a comprehensive nuclear-weapon-test prohibition fell on deaf ears.

The non-nuclear-weapon States tried to raise visibility of the nuclear disarmament issues. Some pursued an amendment conference of the Partial Test-Ban Treaty to convert it into a Comprehensive Test Ban Treaty (CTBT) as a means of promoting public awareness of the dangers of a continued nuclear arms race. Others refused to endorse the conclusions of the NPT's five-year review unless a CTBT was specifically mentioned. Still others requested an advisory opinion from the International Court of Justice regarding the legality of the use or threat of use of nuclear weapons. Some continued to insist on the conclusion of a treaty prohibiting those weapons of mass destruction. After all, the international community had already banned biological and chemical weapons through multilateral treaties, why not nuclear weapons as well?

In 1996 the CTBT was finally concluded. Unfortunately, it contains a provision for its entry into force that is reminiscent of the conditions set forth by the Baruch Plan fifty years earlier in order to proceed to a nuclear-weapons-free world. The CTBT must be ratified by the world's 44 nations that have nuclear-related activities. That is the bad news. The good news is that the five nuclear-weapon States that have signed the NPT are abiding by the CTBT's provisions.

In 2009, the international community has come full circle. United Nations General Assembly resolution 1946 contained

New Russian Government Policy Allows Use of Nuclear Weapons After Conventional Weapons Attacks

Russian President Vladimir Putin signed a new government policy for nuclear deterrence on Tuesday that allows the use of nuclear weapons in response to conventional arms attacks.

Russia says its nuclear weapons are developed in order to deter potential attacks and can be used to combat a strike targeting the nation's critical government and military infrastructure, according to government policy.

The decree Putin signed on Tuesday replaces a 10-year-old document that expired this year. It outlines the types of threats that could trigger Russia's use of atomic weapons—including an attack with conventional, non-nuclear weapons that "threatens the existence" of the country.

The new policy says that if the government obtains "reliable information" about the launch of ballistic missiles targeting Russia or its allies, a nuclear response is permissible.

the basic elements of a nuclear-weapons-free world: a general commitment to the elimination of nuclear weapons and an internationally-acceptable and verifiable system to promote the peaceful uses of atomic energy. After more than six decades of nuclear proliferation—both horizontal as well as vertical—the world seems poised to implement those same basic elements. As in 1946, the U.S. is expected to take the lead.

Public officials in some countries have begun to consider what a world without nuclear weapons would look like. The UN Secretary-General has detailed a five-point proposal.[2] The UK has put forward its ideas in this regard.[3] A number of former political leaders in and out of the U.S. have enlivened the debate with calls for the elimination of nuclear weapons.[4]

The new administration in Washington has begun to bring about some important changes in international relations. During

In addition, the document specifies that atomic weapons can be used under the condition of "enemy impact on critically important government or military facilities of the Russian Federation, the incapacitation of which could result in the failure of retaliatory action of nuclear forces."

The New START agreement—a nuclear arms reduction treaty between the U.S. and Russia was signed by former Presidents Barack Obama and Dmitry Medvedev in 2010. It is the last remaining U.S.-Russia arms control deal after the Trump administration withdrew from the 1987 Intermediate-Range Nuclear Forces treaty last week.

The Obama-era treaty, which limits each country to no more than 1,550 deployed nuclear warheads and 700 deployed missiles and bombers, is set to expire next February.

The Trump administration reportedly plans to resume arms-control talks with Russia, including on the New START treaty, but the U.S. wants China to be involved in any new pact. Moscow, however, has said Beijing taking part in a nuclear treaty with Washington is not feasible, according to an Associated Press report.

"Russia OKs Use of Nukes in Response to Non-Nuclear Attacks," by Erika Williams, Courthouse News Service, June 2, 2020.

last year's presidential campaign, then Senator Barack Obama called for a world in which there are no nuclear weapons, adding that to get there would not entail unilateral disarmament but a continuing commitment under the NPT on the long road towards eliminating them.[5] Once in office, President Obama reiterated his general commitment to the elimination of nuclear weapons. That was one of the basic tenets of the 1946 General Assembly resolution. In his speech in Prague, on 5 April 2009, President Obama described the path to a nuclear-weapons-free world.[6] He began by stating what many believe: "The existence of thousands of nuclear weapons is the most dangerous legacy of the Cold War." He then added:

> Today, the Cold War has disappeared but thousands of those weapons have not. In a strange turn of history, the threat of global nuclear war has gone down, but the risk of a nuclear attack has gone up. More nations have acquired these weapons. Testing has continued. Black markets trade in nuclear secrets and nuclear materials. The technology to build a bomb has spread. Terrorists are determined to buy, build or steal one. Our efforts to contain these dangers are centred on a global non-proliferation regime, but as more people and nations break the rules, we could reach the point where the centre cannot hold.

Admitting that the goal of a nuclear-weapons-free world would not be easy to achieve, he then described the steps the United States was ready to take:

- reduce the role of nuclear weapons in its national security strategy
- negotiate a new Strategic Arms Reduction Treaty (START) with Russia this year to reduce warheads and stockpiles
- ratify the CTBT
- conclude a treaty that verifiably ends the production of fissile materials intended for use in nuclear weapons
- strengthen the NPT as a basis for cooperation in the peaceful uses of nuclear energy
- ensure that terrorists never acquire a nuclear weapon

- promote a new international effort to secure all vulnerable nuclear material around the world within four years.

President Obama has made a bold proposal for the elimination of nuclear weapons. If nothing else, he has put nuclear disarmament on the international agenda. A long debate and complicated negotiations will follow, but the U.S. has shown a willingness to lead and, even more important, to set an example. The START proposal is a case in point.

Fortunately, the Russian Federation seems to be a willing partner in this first stage. Moscow and Washington must reduce their own arsenals before asking others to do the same. Yet, there is bound to be much foot dragging among some of the other nuclear-weapon States. In that regard, the U.S. will also have to point the way in its nuclear posture review. Significant changes in its official nuclear policy could translate into a new nuclear posture for the North Atlantic Treaty Organization. The nuclear-weapon States and their allies must abandon the way they now relate to nuclear weapons.

Another question which President Obama did not mention is the degree to which his proposals will encounter resistance within his own country, especially among groups most interested in the maintenance of the nuclear status quo, beginning with the nuclear laboratories themselves. In the U.S., as elsewhere in the nuclear-weapon States, these have grown accustomed to receiving funding from the national defense budget. The development, effectiveness and safety of nuclear weapons are their livelihood, which they have resisted to surrender in the past.

Six decades ago it might have been easier to achieve a nuclear-weapons-free world, but now it will take an enlightened leadership to do so.

Notes

1. Bernard Baruch, the US representative to the UN Atomic Energy Commission, submitted the proposal on 14 June 1946 and stated in part:

"The United States proposes the creation of an International Atomic
Development Authority, to which should be entrusted all phases of the
development and use of atomic energy..
"We of this nation, desirous of helping to bring peace to the world and realizing
the heavy obligations upon us arising from our possession of the means
of producing the bomb and from the fact that it is part of our armament,
are prepared to make our full contribution toward effective control of
atomic energy.
"When an adequate system for control of atomic energy, including the
renunciation of the bomb as a weapon, has been agreed upon and put
into effective operation and condign punishments set up for violations of
the rules of control which are to be stigmatized as international crimes,
we propose that:
- Manufacture of atomic bombs shall stop;
- Existing bombs shall be disposed of pursuant to the terms of the treaty; and
- The Authority shall be in possession of full information as to the know-how for
the production of atomic energy."
2. "The United Nations and security in a nuclear-weapon-free world," 24 October 2008.
3. "Lifting the Nuclear Shadow: Creating the Conditions for Abolishing Nuclear
Weapons", a Policy information Paper by the Foreign and Commonwealth Office,
4 February 2009.
4. For example, George P. Shultz, William J. Perry, Henry A. Kissinger and Sam Nunn, "A
World Free of Nuclear Weapons," and "Toward a Nuclear-Free World," Wall Street
Journal, 4 January 2007 and 15 January 2008.
5. His proposals were the most sweeping put forward by a presidential candidate except
for Congressman Dennis J. Kucinich's call for the abolition of nuclear weapons.
6. The White House, www.whitehouse.gov.
7. On 1 April 2009 Presidents Obama and Medvedev agreed in London to pursue such
an agreement.

> *"If comprehensive verification measures are included and relations among countries improve, the TPNW may be foundational in the process of disarming and dismantling nuclear weapons globally in the future."*

Treaties Can Help Bring an End to Nuclear Proliferation

Atomic Heritage Foundation

In this viewpoint, the Atomic Heritage Foundation takes a close look at the Treaty on the Prohibition of Nuclear Weapons (TPNW), which the United Nations passed in July 2017. While 122 countries adopted this treaty and 70 had signed it at the time this viewpoint was originally published in 2019, countries with nuclear weapons resisted signing the TPNW. Additionally, the treaty will not enter into force until at least 50 countries have ratified it, and as of 2019 only 22 countries had done so. However, non-nuclear weapons states have consistently pressured nuclear weapons states to sign and ratify the agreement. The TPNW democratized the issue of nuclear weapons and focuses on their humanitarian impacts, and it can be amended to become more effective. The Atomic Heritage Foundation is a nonprofit organization in Washington, DC, dedicated to the preservation and interpretation of the Manhattan Project and the Atomic Age and its legacy.

"The Treaty on the Prohibition of Nuclear Weapons," Atomic Heritage Foundation, December 8, 2017. Updated April 3, 2019. Reprinted by permission. Courtesy of the Atomic Heritage Foundation.

As you read, consider the following questions:

1. What are the Humanitarian Initiative's three main arguments against the use of nuclear weapons?
2. What are some of the limitations of the TPNW listed in this viewpoint?
3. What does Dr. Jürgen Scheffran suggest could make the TPNW effective?

On July 7, 2017, the United Nations passed Resolution 71/258, or the Treaty on the Prohibition of Nuclear Weapons (TPNW). 122 nations adopted this ambitious treaty to prohibit the development, testing, production, manufacturing, acquisition, and possession of nuclear weapons and nuclear explosives.[1] After it passed, initially 23 countries signed the treaty when it was first opened for signature on September 20, 2017. Since then, 47 additional countries have signed the treaty.[2]

Notably and unsurprisingly, the countries that did not sign the TPNW are countries with nuclear weapons. The 5 nuclear states that are party to the Nuclear Nonproliferation Treaty (NPT) which are the United States, Russia, China, the United Kingdom, and France, and the nuclear states outside of the NPT (India, Pakistan, Israel, and North Korea), boycotted the vote. As well, countries under the U.S. nuclear umbrella did not vote. For example, Japan, South Korea, and NATO members do not possess nuclear weapons but they are under the protection of the United States through extended deterrence.

The TPNW will not enter into force until at least 50 countries have ratified it. While 70 countries have signed the treaty and thus indicated that they accept it and promise not to undermine it, these signatures are not legally binding. Ratification is legally binding because the treaty must be adopted by the countries' legislatures and therefore become part of those countries' laws.[3] As of February 2019, only 22 countries have ratified the TPNW and became state parties to the treaty, including Austria, Costa Rica, Mexico, and

New Zealand.[4] This means that the treaty does not yet have legal force and effect.[5] The TPNW will enter into force 90 days after 50 countries ratify it.

The Humanitarian Initiative

The TPNW has its roots in the Humanitarian Initiative, which is "a continuation of the decades-long drive to advance nuclear disarmament through legal means" and aims to "'[fill] the legal gap' on the use of nuclear weapons and advancing the nuclear disarmament agenda."[6]Countries that support the Initiative have pointed to three core arguments for prohibiting nuclear weapons:[7]

1. There have been too many "close calls" that almost resulted in the use of nuclear weapons.

2. The humanitarian and environmental impacts of a nuclear detonation would be catastrophic, and no nation has the capacity to respond to such a situation.

3. The use of nuclear weapons would inherently violate the idea of just wars and, in particular, *Jus in Bello* (Latin for "right in war"), which refers to the actions of parties in armed conflicts.[8] The theory of just wars states that for a country to act morally in a war or conflict, it must follow the principles of discrimination (only attacking combatants and not attacking innocent, nonmilitary civilians), proportionality (a country's force used in war must be proportional to the country's adversary's use of force), and responsibility (ensuring that all actions are carried out with the intention of producing only good impacts, negative impacts of action are not intended, and "the good of the war must outweigh the damage done by it").[9]

The inception of the Humanitarian Initiative began after the 2010 UN NPT Review Conference. The 2010 Review Conference stated in the final document that:

"The Conference expresses its deep concern at the catastrophic humanitarian consequences of any use of nuclear weapons and reaffirms the need for all States at all times to comply with applicable international law, including international humanitarian law."[10]

This was the first time that the humanitarian consequences of nuclear weapons have been taken into consideration during an NPT Review Conference.

From 2013 to 2014, three inter-governmental conferences were held in Norway, Mexico, and Austria about the humanitarian consequences of nuclear weapons. As well, NGOs had the opportunity to bring in civil society's perspective on nuclear issues and played an instrumental role in these conferences. The most prominent NGO was the International Campaign to Abolish Nuclear Weapons (ICAN). The December 2014 Vienna Conference resulted in the Humanitarian Pledge, which "[r]ecogniz[ed] the complexity of and interrelationship between these consequences [of nuclear weapons] on health, environment, infrastructure, food security, climate, development, social cohesion and the global economy that are systemic and potentially irreversible."[11]

At the 2015 NPT Review Conference, Switzerland, on behalf of 16 other countries, delivered a joint statement about the "humanitarian consequences" and the "immeasurable suffering" a nuclear explosion would bring. The statement concludes that "[a]ll States must intensify their efforts to outlaw nuclear weapons and achieve a world free of nuclear weapons."[12] Eventually, a total of 159 countries signed onto this declaration.[13]

In 2016, a special UN working group was convened to discuss the possibility of nuclear disarmament. In August of that year, the group focused on the legal frameworks surrounding nuclear weapons and later proposed that negotiations for a treaty prohibiting nuclear weapons should take place. This proposition eventually led to the December 2016 UN General Assembly Resolution 71/258, or the TPNW.[14]

Nuclear Weapons States and the Vienna Conference

For the first time in December 2014, nuclear-weapon states that are party to the NPT attended the conference on the Humanitarian Impact of Nuclear Weapons: The United States and the United Kingdom. China, also an NPT member, sent an unofficial representative. India and Pakistan, two nuclear-weapon states that are not part of the NPT, were also present and had attended previous conferences.[15] The agenda of this Vienna Conference focused on "the risk of nuclear weapons use, the application of international law to the consequences of nuclear weapons explosions, and the shortfalls in international capacity to address a humanitarian emergency caused by the use of nuclear weapons."[16]

Austria, in its address, stated that nuclear-weapon states in the NPT needed to "identify and pursue effective measures to fill the legal gap for the prohibition and elimination of nuclear weapons" and promised "to cooperate with all stakeholders to achieve this goal."[17] The United States agreed with this sentiment, but added the caveat that there needs to be "a practical way to do it."[18] The other four nuclear-weapon states in the NPT concurred that there are "serious consequences of nuclear weapon use" but also advocated for "the practical, step-by-step approach [the United States, the United Kingdom, France, Russia, and China] are taking has proven to be the most effective means to increase stability and reduce nuclear dangers."[19]

The conference concluded that there was a legal gap with regards to nuclear weapons and called for a complete and immediate ban on nuclear weapons.[20] This, of course, stood in contradiction of the calls for "the practical, step-by-step approach" to nuclear disarmament. Traditionally, the step-by-step approach took the form of arms control treaties between the United States and Russia. From the end of the Cold War to today, the number of nuclear weapons dropped from over 57,000 weapons to 9,100 between the two countries as a result of these treaties.[21] Since then, however, nuclear arms reduction has slowed down, a situation many non-nuclear weapon states have expressed displeasure with. Furthermore, Washington and Moscow continue their modernization programs, which extend the lives of aging weapons.

Because of this diverging point of view on how to disarm, the United States, the United Kingdom, France, Russia, and China eventually boycotted the UN Working Group that worked on the TPNW and the vote on the TPNW. Allies under the protection of the U.S. nuclear umbrella did the same.

Role of Nongovernmental Organizations

One of the most notable aspects of the TPNW is the role that nongovernmental organizations and civil society played in the writing and eventual adoption of the treaty by the UN. ICAN, a nongovernmental organization that is committed to the prohibition of nuclear weapons, was one of the most prominent organizations in lobbying for the treaty. For its work, the Nobel Committee awarded ICAN the Nobel Peace Prize in 2017, citing "its work to draw attention to the catastrophic humanitarian consequences of any use of nuclear weapons and for its ground-breaking efforts to achieve a treaty-based prohibition of such weapons."[22]

Other NGOs involved in advocating for a ban on nuclear weapons include the International Committee of the Red Cross and the Red Crescent, the International Physicians for the Prevention of Nuclear War, and the Women's International League for Peace and Freedom.

Strengths of TPNW

The TPNW has two notable strengths. First, it "democratized" nuclear weapons issues. Second, it focused on the humanitarian impacts of nuclear weapons by highlighting the stories of survivors.

The conferences leading up to the treaty and the UN negotiations made nuclear weapons issues more democratic on two fronts. First, non-nuclear weapon states, such as Norway, Austria, Switzerland, Mexico, and Brazil, had the opportunity to take the lead on writing and negotiating a UN resolution related to nuclear weapons. Second, civil society played a huge role in the TPNW's adoption. Traditionally, nuclear weapons states have taken the lead and almost monopolized the conversation surrounding nuclear weapons. This started with the failed Baruch Plan (1946), introduced by the United States, to completely eliminate the atomic bomb. This democratization demonstrated that concerns around nuclear weapons are not only limited to states that possess them.

Another strength is that the TPNW specifically puts front and center the victims of nuclear weapons and nuclear weapons testing. By doing so, the Humanitarian Initiative was reminding everyone about the real costs and consequences of nuclear weapons. During the conferences, survivors had the opportunity to share their stories. For example, Setsuko Thurlow, a *hibakusha* (atomic bomb survivor) from Hiroshima, has been a leader in ICAN and has shared her story to make real the consequences of nuclear weapons.[23] As well, Indigenous communities in Australia had the opportunity to present their statement before the UN about the impacts of British tests on their community, health, and culture. [24] While the Limited Test Ban Treaty of 1963 was, in part, a response to the Castle Bravo test, which resulted in the *Daigo Fukuryu Maru* Incident and the Marshallese being exposed to radioactive fallout, the language of the LTBT itself does not address the humanitarian impacts of atmospheric testing.

Limitations of TPNW

The TPNW faces crucial limitations that must be addressed in order to ensure its success. The most notable problem is verification, which typically refers to "technical means and measures designed to ensure that a country is following the terms of the treaty and that it is not liable to engage in deception or outright cheating in an attempt to circumvent the spirit and the letter of the agreement."[25]

Many practitioners and arms control scholars have noted that verification is the "most crucial but also the most difficult to negotiate."[26] Verification is critical, because it establishes trust among countries and ensures that all parties are compliant with the treaty they signed. However, when a country is willing to undergo a verification process as part of its treaty obligations, that country must be willing to give up a certain level of secrecy and privacy. A verification process that reveals too much information may put that country's security at risk. For that reason, negotiating verification procedures is the most difficult part.

Unlike the Chemical Weapons Convention of 1993, the TPNW does not include a verification or compliance regime to ensure that a nuclear weapons state is in compliance with its obligations to eliminate its nuclear stockpile. Beyond mentioning that an international organization would oversee the dismantlement and disarmament verification of nuclear weapons,[27] it does not outline the duties and responsibilities of said organization, nor does it detail the types of verification procedures a nuclear weapons state would have to undergo (e.g., on-site inspections).

As part of the TPNW, state parties must also be in compliance with the International Atomic Energy Association (IAEA) Safeguards Agreement. The Safeguards Agreement allow the IAEA to verify that a country with a nuclear energy program is not using its energy program for nuclear-weapons purposes and that the country is upholding its nonproliferation commitments.[28]However, the IAEA strictly deals with the issues of nuclear energy and therefore cannot oversee the dismantlement and disarmament of nuclear weapons.

As Dr. Jürgen Scheffran, a physicist and professor of geography at the University of Hamburg, Germany, states:

> To be effective, the TPNW needs to be adequately verified to build confidence, assure compliance of the State Parties and provide timely warning of non-compliance. Preconditions in the verification process are to define the goals, indicated by legal requirements regarding treaty-limited items and activities, and to identify the means to monitor states and activities. Goals and means of verification need to be balanced in terms of its benefits, costs and risks. The question is whether an intolerable deviation from treaty, limited items, and activities can be detected with reasonable efforts."[29]

Future of the TPNW

The TPNW is not, by any means, immutable. Like other treaties, it can be amended to improve its effectiveness.

Dr. Scheffran suggests an adaptive approach to amending the TPNW and outlines three basic points that future amendments should include. First is preventing party states from accessing "any nuclear weapons, nuclear materials or other components relevant for a nuclear weapons capability."[30] To accomplish this, states parties would participate in information exchanges and data gathering, which include but are not limited to declarations, on-site inspections, and remote monitoring.[31] Second is detecting illicit nuclear activities and preventing the (re)armament of state parties. Third is to create plans that include the "active dismantlement of nuclear weapons, disposal of nuclear materials, and the conversion or destruction of nuclear facilities."[32]

Dr. Scheffran ends his recommendations by pointing out the importance that the current political climate and the relationships with other nations play in countries' acquisition of–and decision to keep–nuclear weapons. He proposes that there should be an implementation of political, organizational, and societal mechanisms outside of the treaty to bolster verification and trust-building measures to reduce the incentives for a country to acquire a nuclear weapon. These mechanisms include bringing the general public into conversations about nuclear issues through education and discourse and improving international conflict-resolution procedures to resolve problems among countries before they become armed conflicts. [33]

Tamara Patton, a PhD Student at the Woodrow Wilson School of Public and International Affairs, suggests her own potential amendments to the TPNW, which would also address the problems surrounding verification. She proposes developing an "of an international monitoring system for nuclear disarmament and nonproliferation verification (NDN-IMS)."[34] The purpose of such a system would be to monitor state parties' compliance with the TPNW, coordinate research to develop technologies that improve verification methods, and increase the warning time for the international community if a country decides to restart its nuclear weapons program after becoming a party to the TPNW. [35]

Conclusion

In the short term, the TPNW remains controversial in its success in prohibiting nuclear weapons. The treaty continues to gain support from states that do not possess nuclear weapons. However, countries that have nuclear weapons argue that they need those weapons to protect themselves against hostile nations and guard against an uncertain future. However, if comprehensive verification measures are included and relations among countries improve, the TPNW may be foundational in the process of disarming and dismantling nuclear weapons globally in the future.

Notes

[1] "Treaty on the Prohibition of Nuclear Weapons" (UN Resolution, New York City, 2017 https://www.un.org/disarmament/wp-content/uploads/2017/10/tpnw-info-kit-v2.pdf), 12.

[2] Signature/ratification status of the Treaty on the Prohibition of Nuclear Weapons," *ICAN*, accessed March 20, 2019, http://www.icanw.org/status-of-the-treaty-on-the-prohibition-of-nuclear-weapons/.

[3] "What is the CTBT?" *CTBTO*, accessed March 25, 2019, https://www.ctbto.org/the-treaty/article-xiv-conferences/2011/afc11-information-for-media-and-press/what-is-the-ctbt/.

[4] Signature/ratification status of the Treaty on the Prohibition of Nuclear Weapons," *ICAN*, accessed March 20, 2019, http://www.icanw.org/status-of-the-treaty-on-the-prohibition-of-nuclear-weapons/.

[5] "Glossary," *United Nations Treaty Collection*, accessed March 20, 2019, https://treaties.un.org/pages/overview.aspx?path=overview/glossary/page1_en.xml.

[6] Michal Onderco, "Why nuclear weapon ban treaty is unlikely to fulfill its promise," *Global Affairs* 3, no. 4-5 (2017): 391.

[7] Ibid., 392.

[8] "What are jus ad bellum and jus in bello?" *ICRC*, published January 22, 2015, https://www.icrc.org/en/document/what-are-jus-ad-bellum-and-jus-bello-0.

[9] "Just War Theory," *Oregon State*, accessed March 20, 2019, https://oregonstate.edu/instruct/phl201/modules/just_war_theory/criteria_intro.html. [10] "Final Document" (2010 Review Conference of the Parties to the Treaty on the Non-Proliferation of Nuclear Weapons, New York City, 2010, https://www.un.org/ga/search/view_doc.asp?symbol=NPT/CONF.2010/50%20%28VOL.I%29), 19.

[11] "Humanitarian Pledge" (Statement, Vienna Conference, Vienna, 2014, http://www.icanw.org/campaign/humanitarian-initiative/).

[12] "Joint Statement on the humanitarian dimension of nuclear disarmament by Austria, Chile, Costa Rica, Denmark, Holy See, Egypt, Indonesia, Ireland, Malaysia, Mexico, New Zealand, Nigeria, Norway, Philippines, South Africa, Switzerland" (Joint Statement, First Session of the Preparatory Committee for the 2015 Review

Conference of the Parties to the Treaty on the Non-Proliferation of Nuclear Weapons, New York City, 2015, http://www.reachingcriticalwill.org/images/documents/Disarmament-fora/npt/prepcom12/statements/2May_IHL.pdf).

[13] "Humanitarian Initiative," *ICAN*, accessed March 20, 2019, http://www.icanw.org/campaign/humanitarian-initiative/.

[14] Ibid.

[15] Kingston Reif, "Nuclear Impact Meeting is Largest Yet," *Arms Control Association*, published January/February 2015, https://www.armscontrol.org/ACT/2015_0102/News/Nuclear-Impact-Meeting-Is-Largest-Yet.

[16] Ibid.

[17] Ibid.

[18] Ibid.

[19] Rebecca Davis Gibbons, "The humanitarian turn in nuclear disarmament and the Treaty on the Prohibition of Nuclear Weapons," *The Nonproliferation Review* 25 (2018):1-2, 11-36.

[20] "A Pledge To Fill The Legal Gap," (Vienna Report, Vienna, 2014, http://www.icanw.org/wp-content/uploads/2012/08/ViennaReport.pdf): 2.

[21] David Wright, "Arms control successes," *Union of Concerned Scientists*, published December 17, 2014, https://blog.ucsusa.org/david-wright/nuclear-weapons-end-of-the-cold-war-769.

[22] "The Nobel Peace Prize for 2017," *The Nobel Prize*, accessed March 22, 2019, https://www.nobelprize.org/prizes/peace/2017/press-release/.

[23] "Setsuko Thurlow," *ICAN*, accessed March 25, 2019, http://www.icanw.org/setsuko-thurlow/.

[24] "Indigenous Statement to the U.N. Nuclear Weapons Ban Treaty Negotiations," *ICAN*, accessed March 25, 2019, http://www.icanw.org/wp-content/uploads/2017/05/Indigenous-Statement-June-2017.pdf.

[25] Craig R. Wuest, "The Challenge for Arms Control Verification in the Post-New START World," (Report, Washington, DC, 2012, https://www.ipndv.org/wp-content/uploads/2012/07/Wuest_2012_The_Challenge_for_Arms_Control_Verification_in_the_Post_New_START_World.pdf): 2.

[26] Michal Onderco, "Why nuclear weapon ban treaty is unlikely to fulfill its promise," *Global Affairs* 3, no. 4-5 (2017): 394.

[27] Ibid.

[28] "Basics of IAEA Safeguards," *IAEA*, accessed March 25, 2019, https://www.iaea.org/topics/basics-of-iaea-safeguards.

[29] Jurgen Scheffran, "Verification and security of transformation to a nuclear weapon-free world: the framework of the Treaty on the Prohibition of Nuclear Weapons," *Global Change, Peace & Security* 30, no. 2 (2018): 145.

[30] Jurgen Scheffran, "Verification and security of transformation to a nuclear weapon-free world: the framework of the Treaty on the Prohibition of Nuclear Weapons," *Global Change, Peace & Security* 30, no. 2 (2018): 147.

[31] Ibid.

[32] Ibid.

[33] Ibid.

[34] Tamara Patton, "An international monitoring system for verification to support both the treaty on the prohibition of nuclear weapons and the nonproliferation treaty," *Global Change, Peace & Security* 30, no.2 (2018): 190.

[35] Ibid.

"The United States' only option to thwart Iran's nuclear ambition is to listen and negotiate towards a durable agreement."

Preventing Iran from Going Nuclear Requires a Change in the U.S.'s Approach

Sumesh Shiwakoty

In this viewpoint, Sumesh Shiwakoty argues that the geopolitical situation has changed considerably between 2015—when the Joint Comprehensive Plan of Action (JPCOA) was first agreed upon by Iran and other countries, including the U.S.—and today. JPCOA stipulated that Iran would start dismantling its nuclear program and allow inspections of nuclear facilities in exchange for billions of dollars in sanction relief. After former President Trump withdrew from JPCOA, Iran moved forward with its pursuit of a nuclear program. Regional power dynamics have changed in the intervening years in Iran's favor, and Iran has managed to enter economic alliances that do not involve the U.S., which have helped develop its economy. As a result, the U.S. will have to try harder to negotiate and build trust if it wants to revitalize a nuclear agreement with Iran. Sumesh Shiwakoty is a policy analyst and commentator.

"Can America Prevent Iran from Going Nuclear?" by Sumesh Shiwakoty, National Interest, February 17, 2022. Reprinted by permission.

As you read, consider the following questions:

1. According to Shiwakoty, what are the two options the United States has in relation to Iran's nuclear program?
2. What does Shiwakoty say would allow the U.S. to have a chance of stopping Iran's nuclear weapons program?
3. According to this viewpoint, how has the U.S.'s position weakened since the signing of JPCOA?

Iran is now closer to acquiring nuclear weapons than ever before. The ongoing nuclear talks in Vienna to revive the 2015 Joint Comprehensive Plan of Action (JCPOA) may be the last chance to stop Iran from becoming a nuclear state, potentially triggering a nuclear arms race in an already unstable region.

The United States has only two options. First, to pursue its current path and witness Iran go nuclear at some point in the near future, even if Teheran agrees to revive JCPOA. Second, to acknowledge that the ground realities have changed, thus necessitating dialogue with Iran about its concerns and making possible concessions.

Ultimately, if the United States is to play a leadership role in the Middle East and wants to stop Iran from acquiring nuclear weapons in the foreseeable future, it will need to embrace the Nuclear Non-Proliferation Treaty (NPT), end its double standards towards Israel's nuclear program, and promote a nuclear-free zone in the Middle East.

2022 Is Not 2015

Realities on the ground have changed dramatically since 2015 and mainly in Iran's favor. Since Donald Trump's withdrawal from JCPOA, before which Iran largely complied with the deal, Iran has breached its commitment and has progressed significantly in its nuclear pursuits. Under the JCPOA, Iran was not allowed to enrich uranium past 3.67 percent. At present, Iran is enriching uranium at 60 percent, which is significantly higher than what is necessary for civilian purposes. International Atomic Energy Agency (IAEA) director-general Raphael Grossi noted recently that only those countries making bombs are enriching uranium at 60 percent.

Moreover, since 2018, Iran has significantly diminished its breakout time—the time needed to have enough enriched uranium make one nuclear weapon—from the one year originally negotiated in the JCPOA to the current three weeks to a few months, as per various reports. Although this estimate is highly subjective, experts broadly agree Iran's breakout time has shortened substantially. As a result, the Iranian leadership seems convinced that they can use the threat of Iranian weaponization to deter any potential military threats, hence assuming the upper hand in negotiations.

U.S. policymakers seem unwilling to acknowledge the change in the regional power dynamics and, in recent days, have repeatedly talked about a "Plan B"—implying military interventions—if negotiations fail. But, with the U.S. midterm elections approaching, President Joe Biden will hesitate to embark on another war in the Middle East, the political support for which has evaporated after the endless and largely failed wars in Iraq and Afghanistan.

The Power Dynamics Have Shifted

In 2015, Iran wanted a deal as much as the United States because international sanctions were crushing Iran's economy. Now, the United States needs a deal more than Iran does. While current sanctions on Iran are detrimental to its economy, Iran may not want the United States to rejoin JCPOA because then the United States could reimpose sanctions via the UN Security Council. After withdrawing from the JCPOA, the Trump administration tried to do just that, but UN secretary-general Antonio Guterres and the remaining parties of JCPOA maintained that since the United States was no longer a party to JCPOA, it could no longer trigger UN sanctions on Iran.

In addition, Iran is moving further outside the U.S. orbit, having received full membership in the Shanghai Cooperation Organization, an alliance whose members include Russia, China,

India, and other emerging markets. This new membership enables Tehran to expand its trade to those emerging economies. Tehran also has recently signed the "Iran-China Comprehensive Strategic Partnership" with Beijing, with China promising investments of $400 billion in Iran, of which $280 billion will be in Iran's energy sector. In return, Iran has agreed to export petroleum to China at a reduced price.

Simultaneously, the U.S. position has weakened since the signing of the JCPOA. As the global reserve status of the U.S. dollar is fraying, the strength of American sanctions is in constant decay as well. According to the International Monetary Fund (IMF), in 2001, the dollar accounted for 72 percent of the world's foreign exchange reserves but only 59 percent today. Moreover, fewer than 20 percent of executives surveyed by McKinsey Global Institute expect the dollar to be the dominant global reserve currency by 2025. In the past, the dollar's reserve status added teeth to the U.S.-led economic sanctions because any country, even those that do not do much business with the United States, need access to the American banking system to clear their payments and manage cash.

But the future of the dollar as a global reserve currency is in danger as it depends mainly on its "Petro currency" status—which resulted from Richard Nixon's 1974 agreement with Saudi king Faisal, where Saudi Arabia promised to accept payment in dollars for most of its oil exports. However, China enjoys new significant leverage over Saudi Arabia as it is now the world's leading importer of crude oil and is pressuring the Saudis to trade oil in yuan. In fact, Saudi Arabia's state-controlled petroleum company, Saudi Aramco, recently indicated it might issue yuan-denominated bonds. Moreover, in recent days, many experts have been concluding that if U.S. policymakers continue to employ dollar-based economic sanctions, it will further exacerbate the dollar's demise as the global reserve currency, pointing out that Washington must strike a delicate balance when considering economic sanctions. Contrarily, Iran is withstanding current sanctions and has successfully resisted Trump's maximum pressure campaign. There now seems to be a broader consensus in the Biden administration that initiating any new sanctions will do little in convincing Iran to veer from its current path.

Barriers of Trust

The United States must convince Iran and the international community that it will abide by the terms of any agreement that is struck. Iran wants assurances that no future U.S. president will withdraw from any nuclear deal—an understandable concern considering Sen. Ted Cruz's comments that "it is a 100% certainty that any future Republican president will tear up" any nuclear deal with Iran. Should Biden achieve an agreement, he must take it to Congress to be ratified as a treaty while his party still enjoys a majority in Congress. Doing so will prevent any future U.S. president from simply withdrawing from the deal by executive order.

As Iran's chief nuclear negotiator in Vienna, Bagheri Kani, stated in reply to U.S. negotiators, "This is about an agreement, not a policy. If there is a peace agreement between two states, it has the effect of a treaty. This is international law. It is not intended that domestic laws of the U.S. can prevail over an international agreement. That is against international law." Further, Biden should work with the international community to create new arbitration mechanisms so that anyone violating the terms of the deal can be held accountable. He must address the fact that many of the sanctions relief promised to Iran in 2015 was never actually implemented due to legal hurdles.

If the United States cannot provide Iran with the assurances it is seeking, it is doubtful that Iranians will see value in agreeing to any potential new deal. With a lack of mutual trust between the United States and Iran, we might see a repeat of what occurred in North Korea in 2007. That year, following the Six-Party Talks, Pyongyang agreed to stop plutonium production and shut down North Korea's major production facilities at Yongbyon in exchange for a promise that the United States would supply North Korea with 500,000 tons of heavy fuel oil, remove Pyongyang from the state sponsors of terrorism list, and terminate the application of the Trading with the Enemy Act. Siegfried S. Hecker, a leading American nuclear scientist who visited North Korean nuclear facilities on multiple occasions, concluded that the disablement actions of Pyongyang "to be serious and in good faith." However, the United States never fulfilled its promise to North Korea, and we are still leaving with the repercussions.

Achieving a Stable Agreement

The United States' only option to thwart Iran's nuclear ambition is to listen and negotiate towards a durable agreement. The United States should work to end Iran's current security dilemma concerns, abide by the spirit of the NPT regime, and pledge to a no-first-use nuclear policy. This in itself diminishes the usage of nuclear weapons from a security perspective and can solve Iran's current security dilemma. Many analysts have noted that nuclear war did not emerge as a serious option throughout all the military standoffs between India and China because both had a no-first-use policy, unlike during tensions between India and Pakistan.

Further, to solve Iran's current security dilemma, the United States should seek a nuclear-free zone in the Middle East. To do that, it must first end its hypocrisy in denying that Israel possesses nuclear weapons. Evidence shows that during the final years of the 1960s, the Central Intelligence Agency had already certified that Israel had developed nuclear warheads. But President Richard Nixon and Israeli prime minister Golda Meir agreed that the United States would not acknowledge that Israel possessed a nuclear arsenal and would not pressure Israel to sign the NPT as long as Israel did not declare itself a nuclear state.

The U.S. government has abided with this deal ever since. Many have argued that this privileged status gives Israel's leadership a sense of power over others as it can enjoy the benefits of becoming a nuclear weapons state without the responsibilities that come with it. But enabling this aberration to exist degrades America's moral standing in the world. Further, there is broad international consensus that the opaqueness of Israel's nuclear program is a critical hurdle in creating a nuclear-free zone in the Middle East, an aspiration that goes back to President George H.W. Bush. U.S. promotion of a nuclear-free zone in the Middle East would address Iran's security concerns and encourage it to remain a part of the NPT regime, unlike Egypt, which withdrew from NPT in 1981 with the condition to rejoin the NPT only after Israel joins.

Iran, for its part, should agree to reverse all its recent progress toward building nuclear weapons, extend its current breakout time to the JCPOA standard of one year or more, and accept strict and verifiable international mechanisms to monitor its compliance.

Many Washington hardliners will smirk at these proposals as being too ambitious and unrealistic. However, given all the advances Iran has made so far on its nuclear program and the technical knowledge it has gained along the way, this situation is headed toward crisis at a blistering pace. If the United States does not address Iran's concerns in order to achieve a negotiated settlement, then the world will have to live with Iran as a nuclear weapons power.

Periodical and Internet Sources Bibliography

The following articles have been selected to supplement the diverse views presented in this chapter.

Naina Bajekal, "She's Spent a Decade Fighting to Ban Nuclear Weapons. The Stakes Are Only Getting Higher," *TIME*, January 4, 2023. https://time.com/6243350/beatrice-fihn-interview-ican-nuclear-war/.

Bill Chappell, "What Happens Now After Russia Suspends the Last Nuclear Arms Treaty with the U.S.?" NPR, February 22, 2023. https://www.npr.org/2023/02/22/1158529106/nuclear-treaty-new-start-putin.

Suzanne Claeys and Alice Spilman, "How Does the Worsening Security Environment Impact Nuclear Disarmament?" Center for Strategic and International Studies, September 13, 2022. https://www.csis.org/analysis/how-does-worsening-security-environment-impact-nuclear-disarmament.

Peter Kenny, "Worldwide Arsenal of Nuclear Weapons Available for Use Rose in 2022, Report Says," Anadolu Agency, March 29, 2023. https://www.aa.com.tr/en/world/worldwide-arsenal-of-nuclear-weapons-available-for-use-rose-in-2022-report-says/2858567.

Daryl Kimball, "U.S.-Russian Nuclear Arms Control Agreements at a Glance," Arms Control Association, October 2022. https://www.armscontrol.org/factsheets/USRussiaNuclearAgreements.

Alexander Kmentt, "The Ban Treaty, Two Years After: A Ray of Hope for Nuclear Disarmament," *Bulletin of the Atomic Scientists*, January 23, 2023. https://thebulletin.org/2023/01/the-ban-treaty-two-years-after-a-ray-of-hope-for-nuclear-disarmament/.

Hans Kristensen and Matt Korda, "The 2022 Nuclear Posture Review: Arms Control Subdued by Military Rivalry," Federation of American Scientists, October 27, 2022. https://fas.org/blogs/security/2022/10/2022-nuclear-posture-review/.

Łukasz Kulesa, "Reinventing Nuclear Disarmament and Nonproliferation as Cooperative Endeavors," Council on Foreign Relations, April 21, 2021. https://www.cfr.org/report/reinventing-nuclear-disarmament-and-nonproliferation-cooperative-endeavors.

Becky Little, "How Survivors of Hiroshima and Nagasaki Organized for Nuclear Disarmament," History, August 5, 2022. https://www.history.com/news/hiroshima-nagasaki-survivors-anti-nuclear-activism.

Steven Pifer, "Three Ways the U.S. Should Respond to Russia's Suspension of New START," *Bulletin of the Atomic Scientists*, March 24, 2023. https://thebulletin.org/2023/03/three-ways-the-us-should-respond-to-russias-suspension-of-new-start/.

Kali Robinson, "What Is the Iran Nuclear Deal?" Council on Foreign Relations, July 20, 2022. https://www.cfr.org/backgrounder/what-iran-nuclear-deal.

OPPOSING
VIEWPOINTS®
SERIES

CHAPTER 4

Is There a Significant Chance of Nuclear War?

Chapter Preface

When considering the likelihood of nuclear war, two concepts commonly come up as arguments for nuclear deterrence: the nuclear taboo and mutually assured destruction. The nuclear taboo means that by knowing the devastating impacts a nuclear attack would have and the massive number of civilian casualties it would cause, countries consider nuclear weapons to be in an entirely different category from other types of weapons and have refrained from using them because of their horrific consequences.

However, the nuclear taboo does not explain why countries have continued to develop and maintain nuclear arsenals despite the fact that nuclear weapons have not been used since the bombings of Hiroshima and Nagasaki in 1945. This is where the concept of mutually assured destruction comes in. Mutually assured destruction (sometimes abbreviated as MAD) means that countries are deterred from using nuclear weapons on their adversaries by the knowledge that their adversaries (or their adversaries' allies) will stage a nuclear attack against them in retaliation. With mutually assured destruction, countries feel that they need to have nuclear weapons in order to deter other countries from using them. Unlike the nuclear taboo, it is a concept that is based on distrust, and some argue that this means it stands in the way of a truly stable and peaceful geopolitical situation.

Although the fact that there hasn't been another nuclear attack since Hiroshima and Nagasaki suggests that at least some form of nuclear deterrence has been effective, some people question if the nuclear taboo and mutually assured destruction are less stable than they seem. In early 2022, Russian President Vladimir Putin first threatened to use nuclear weapons in Russia's war with Ukraine and has since continued to make the threat.[1] While some experts say it is unlikely that Russia will actually use them, they also assert that making these kinds of threats can cause the nuclear taboo to deteriorate. Additionally, the number of close calls that have occurred—most notably the Cuban Missile Crisis in 1962, though there have been many others—suggests that mutually assured destruction may not be enough.

The viewpoints in this chapter consider the nuclear taboo, mutually assured destruction, and the state of nuclear deterrence today. They present arguments for why current efforts at nuclear deterrence may or may not be enough to prevent a nuclear attack.

Notes

1. Andrew Roth, Shaun Walker, Jennifer Rankin, and Julian Borger, "Putin Signals Escalation as He Puts Russia's Nuclear Force on High Alert," the *Guardian*, February 27, 2022. https://www.theguardian.com/world/2022/feb/27/vladimir-putin-puts-russia-nuclear-deterrence-forces-on-high-alert-ukraine.

> *"These constraints are known collectively as the 'nuclear taboo,' an informal but widely-observed prohibition made up of moral, political, bureaucratic, military, practical, and diplomatic hurdles and inhibitions."*

The Nuclear Taboo Helps Prevent Nuclear War, but It's Not as Stable as It Used to Be

William Burr and Jeffrey Kimball

In this viewpoint, William Burr and Jeffrey Kimball explain how the nuclear taboo originated after the atomic bombings of Hiroshima and Nagasaki by the U.S. in 1945. The nuclear taboo is an informal prohibition of first use of nuclear weapons. The atomic bombings of Hiroshima and Nagasaki made clear the extensive damage and civilian casualties that would be caused by the weapon, and a nuclear taboo has existed in the decades since. However, the fact that the U.S., Russia, and other countries maintain nuclear arsenals suggests that their use hasn't been entirely ruled out. William Burr is a senior analyst at George Washington University's National Security Archive, where he directs its Nuclear Documentation Project. Jeffrey Kimball is a professor of history at Miami University.

"Seven Decades After Hiroshima, Is There Still a Nuclear Taboo?" by William Burr and Jeffrey Kimball, Bulletin of the Atomic Scientists, August 4, 2015. Reprinted by permission.

As you read, consider the following questions:

1. What was former President Eisenhower's attitude toward nuclear weapons when he assumed office? How did it change over time?
2. What was former President Nixon's "madman theory"?
3. What was the last U.S. nuclear alert of the Cold War?

Seventy years ago, in August 1945, the United States destroyed Hiroshima and Nagasaki with atomic weapons. Since then, neither the United States nor any other nuclear-armed country has used such weapons against an adversary. Why not? During the Cold War, Washington and Moscow made nuclear threats that could have led to catastrophe, and the history of U.S. strategy and policy since 1945 includes many examples of risky nuclear bluster. But it also includes a number of cases in which decision-makers stopped short of nuclear use because of constraints against first use. These constraints are known collectively as the "nuclear taboo," an informal but widely-observed prohibition made up of moral, political, bureaucratic, military, practical, and diplomatic hurdles and inhibitions. This taboo has played an important role in preventing nuclear war. But even though it persists today, it may not be enough to prevent nuclear war in the future.

When the United States dropped atomic bombs on Japan in 1945, top U.S. officials mainly thought of the weapon as a gigantic explosive device with powerful blast effects and were unaware of other dangers, such as radiation poisoning and fallout hazards. But the terrible effects of the weapon and the massive civilian casualties soon made it evident that the bomb was unique in other foreboding ways. Belatedly recognizing what the United States had wrought, President Harry Truman stopped the atomic bombings as Japan was preparing to surrender, telling his cabinet that the "thought of killing another 100,000 people was too horrible" and that he did not like the idea of killing "all those kids."

The atomic bombings had a tremendous impact on international opinion and produced constraints against nuclear use, which U.S. government officials had to take into account. Although U.S. military leaders considered using nuclear weapons against North Korean and Chinese forces, they were unable to identify practical military targets, and global public opinion by that point constrained their use. In November 1950, for example, as U.S.-led United Nations forces retreated in the face of Chinese entry into the Korean War, Truman administration officials debated the merits of attacking China with atomic weapons without UN approval. State Department planning adviser John K. Emmerson objected, arguing in a memo to Dean Rusk (who would later become secretary of state) that "the moral position of the United States would be seriously damaged." Such action "would be deplored and denounced by a considerable number of nations who had up to that time supported the action in Korea. … Should the next atomic bomb be dropped on an Asiatic population, it is easy for foresee the revulsion of feeling which would spread throughout Asia."

Dismayed by the civilian casualties caused by atomic bombs in Japan and later by the incomprehensible destructiveness of hydrogen bombs, as demonstrated by U.S. and Soviet thermonuclear tests, Truman had come to regard both as "weapons of last resort." But his successor Dwight D. Eisenhower thought otherwise, believing that nuclear weapons could be used "just exactly as you would use a bullet or anything else," as he said at a 1955 news conference. After the Korean War ended, Eisenhower and Secretary of State John Foster Dulles claimed they had secretly and successfully brought China to terms at the negotiating table by threatening to use nuclear weapons. In 1954, during the French War in Indochina, Eisenhower and Dulles considered using atomic bombs to break the Viet Minh siege at Dien Bien Phu. They also issued public nuclear threats and placed nuclear (as well as conventional) forces on high readiness during the Taiwan Strait crises of the 1950s. During the 1958 civil war in Lebanon between pro-Western Christians and Soviet-endorsed pan-Arab Muslims, Eisenhower put U.S. nuclear forces on their largest and highest alert yet, with hundreds of strategic bombers readied for launch.

Yet even as Soviet nuclear forces grew and as Eisenhower and Dulles became more aware of nuclear dangers, their thinking shifted. During the 1958 Taiwan Strait Crisis, Eisenhower kept tight control over nuclear weapons and conceded in a message to the British foreign secretary that when you use nuclear weapons "you cross a completely different line." Eisenhower came to view these weapons as belonging in a special category—although he continued to profess support for their use in the event of a Soviet onslaught against Western Europe or an attack against U.S. territory.

The doubts of civilian leaders notwithstanding, in the 1950s the U.S. Air Force drafted war plans that included the preemptive use of nuclear weapons against Soviet bomber and missile bases if U.S. intelligence agencies surmised that the Soviet Union was preparing a surprise attack on U.S. military forces and cities. Preemption continued to be a central tenet in U.S. planning during the Cold War and served as a key justification for increased spending on nuclear weapons.

Secretary of Defense Robert McNamara, who served under Presidents John F. Kennedy and Lyndon B. Johnson, advised against first use of nuclear weapons, except in the instance of massive attacks on U.S. forces abroad by China or the Soviet Union. Both presidents took heed of that advice, although Kennedy brought his country perilously close to the nuclear brink during the Cuban Missile Crisis, when U.S. nuclear forces were at their highest state of alert ever. Luckily, both Kennedy and Soviet Leader Nikita Khrushchev avoided fatal mistakes despite the potential for danger inherent in anti-submarine maneuvers and secret Soviet nuclear deployments.

When challenger Senator Barry Goldwater and others called for the use of nuclear weapons in Vietnam during the 1964 presidential campaign, President Johnson explicitly cited the language of taboo: "For 19 perilous years no nation has loosed the atom against another. To do so … would lead us down an uncertain path of blows and counterblows whose outcome none may know." A CIA study about potential outcomes of nuclear use in Vietnam argued that it would cause a "fundamental revulsion that the U.S. had broken the 20-year taboo on the use of nuclear weapons" and produce a "wave of fear and anger," with allies condemning the United States for "having dragged the world into a new and terrible phase of history." Such admonitions put a damper on any serious White House consideration of using nuclear weapons in Vietnam during Johnson's tenure, although some advisers entertained the notion.

The election of Richard M. Nixon to the presidency, however, brought to power a politician steeped in the Eisenhower-Dulles school of nuclear threat making, who believed that such threats had brought the Korean War to an end. Nixon entered the White House in 1969, while the Vietnam War was raging. Like his national security adviser, Henry Kissinger, he believed that ending it was their top priority, in part because his re-election depended on it. He thought that the right combination of carrots (diplomatic inducements) and sticks (threats and stronger military measures) could make that possible.

Drawing on his experience as vice president during the Eisenhower administration, Nixon had developed what he called the "madman theory," which posited that threatening massive, even excessive, levels of military violence, including nuclear attacks, would intimidate the North Vietnamese and their patrons in the Soviet Union into submission at the negotiating table. During his first year in office he made secret madman threats against North Vietnam in hopes of bringing it into compliance by the end of 1969. He and Kissinger also hoped that such threats would make Soviet leaders worry that the war was going to spin out of control, thus encouraging them to put pressure on Hanoi to make the requisite concessions.

In September 1969, Kissinger's aides drew up a concept plan for military escalation against North Vietnam that included proposals to use nuclear weapons on two railroad lines to China and three mountain passes on the Laos-North Vietnam border. In early October, however, Nixon decided against escalation, in part because of his concerns about negative public reactions at home and abroad and worries about previously scheduled anti-Vietnam War demonstrations. He also faced opposition to escalation from within his own administration, including cautionary advice from some of Kissinger's own aides. Moreover, madman threat-making had not moved Moscow to cooperate in putting pressure on Hanoi to yield in the Paris negotiations.

Instead of escalating militarily, on October 9, 1969, Nixon and Kissinger instructed the Pentagon to place U.S. nuclear and other military forces around the globe on alert, and to do so secretly. Angry that Moscow had not put pressure on Hanoi to back down but instead continued to provide North Vietnam with military aid, Nixon made a last-ditch gambit to get Soviet cooperation. For 18 days in October, the Pentagon orchestrated one of the largest and most extensive secret military operations in U.S. history. Tactical and strategic bomber forces went on alert, as did Polaris missile-launching submarines (intercontinental ballistic missiles were already on high alert routinely). Aircraft carriers made unusual movements in the North Atlantic and Sea of Japan, while destroyers shadowed Soviet merchant ships heading toward North Vietnam. This "Joint Chiefs Readiness Test," as it was called, officially culminated in a flight of nuclear-armed B-52 bombers over northern Alaska, the first time that the Strategic Air Command had undertaken nuclear overflights since a major accident in Greenland in early 1968.

The secret U.S. nuclear alert, though certainly noticed by Soviet leaders, failed to pressure them into helping Nixon win concessions from Hanoi. Instead, Nixon shifted his Vietnam War strategy to a "long route" approach that emphasized unilateral U.S. troop withdrawals, the training and enlargement of South Vietnamese forces, and protracted negotiations designed to achieve a compromise settlement by the time of the 1972 presidential election in the United States.

In the spring of 1972, North Vietnam upset Nixon's plans with a powerful offensive in South Vietnam. White House tapes reveal that at a critical moment in April, when Nixon spoke with Kissinger in the Executive Office Building about the bombing and mining campaign launched in retaliation for the North Vietnamese offensive, Nixon raised the issue of whether they should also bomb dikes along the Red River. When Kissinger complained that such a move would kill large numbers of people, Nixon brought up the option of a nuclear strike: "I'd rather use a nuclear bomb. Have you got that ready?" In response, Kissinger muttered, "Now that, I think, would just be, uh, too much, uh —." Nixon interrupted, "A nuclear bomb, does that bother you?" In a barely understandable retort, Kissinger seemed to say: "A nuclear bomb, you wouldn't do it anyway." Nixon gruffly ended the conversation on this topic, saying, "I just want you to think big, Henry, for Christ's sake!"

His anger notwithstanding, Nixon never took this idea any further, although he brought it up on several other occasions before and after. One of Kissinger's responses in the Executive Office Building conversation suggested what the constraints were: nuclear use would be "too much," as if crossing a line, which would elicit condemnation around the world and provoke Soviet and Chinese responses. Nixon faced the same checks previous presidents had.

Nevertheless, Nixon and Kissinger did not give up on madman threats, nuclear or otherwise. During the 1970 Jordan crisis, they used massive naval deployments to deter what they saw as a Soviet-backed Syrian intervention. In the 1973 Arab-Israeli war, Kissinger instructed the Pentagon to go into defense readiness condition (DEFCON) 3, putting the Strategic Air Command on the highest alert level since the Cuban Missile Crisis in 1962 in order to prevent what he misperceived as the possibility of Soviet intervention. (Nixon was out of action at that moment, inebriated and in despair over Vice President Spiro Agnew's resignation and the unfolding Watergate investigation.)

The DEFCON 3 in 1973 was the last U.S. nuclear alert of the Cold War. The Soviets did not respond with their own readiness measures, but they were angry and irritated. Kissinger, however, came to recognize that threat diplomacy was becoming too dangerous and too incredible to be taken seriously by an adversary. As he explained after he left office, the United States could not "afford to repeat the rapid escalation gambit." Nevertheless, dangerous launch-on-warning and preemptive options remained basic elements in U.S. nuclear planning.

Although subsequent U.S. presidents tacitly ruled out nuclear alerts in the last years of the Cold War, tensions with the Soviet Union often remained high, generating episodes that had the potential to spin out of control. The Soviet reaction to the NATO military exercise of November 1983, code-named Able Archer, was particularly noteworthy. The Soviets interpreted NATO's practice nuclear-weapons release procedures as a portent of actual nuclear-weapons use. Worried about the possibility of a U.S. strike, Moscow readied its nuclear forces. Ultimately, cooler heads prevailed, but November 1983 was an especially tense period in Cold War history. Bellicose talk by President Ronald Reagan and officials in his administration in the months preceding Able Archer about fighting and winning a nuclear war with the Soviet Union had set the stage for the November scare.

The likelihood of deliberate nuclear use by the United States faded as the nuclear taboo became central to the worldview of policymakers, but nuclear threats remained in the playbook of top officials. During the 1991 Persian Gulf War, senior members in President George H. W. Bush's administration declared that nuclear weapons were "taboo" and "unusable" and that employing them would cause Washington to "lose the moral high ground," among other considerations. Nevertheless, other officials floated implicit warnings that could be construed as nuclear threats. Chairman of the Joint Chiefs of Staff Colin Powell, for example, declared that if the Iraqis used chemical or biological weapons, the American people would require "vengeance," and said that they "have the means to extract it."

The language of nuclear threat-making continued to pepper discussions about foreign policy, especially during the lead-up to the 2003 U.S. invasion of Iraq and in debates over the Iranian nuclear program. In early 2002, President George W. Bush set the tone when he declared that "all options are on the table" to counter threats by other states who would use "weapons of mass destruction" against the United States. Responding to reporters' questions three years later in Brussels about U.S. policy toward Iran's nuclear program, President Bush responded with what many regarded as a typical Bushism: "This notion that the United States is getting ready to attack Iran is simply ridiculous. And having said that, all options are on the table." He was not alone. Leading Democrats, including then-senators Hillary Clinton, John Edwards, and Barack Obama, used similar language.

As a presidential candidate and as president, however, Obama promised to reduce the role and number of nuclear weapons in the U.S. arsenal. He called for "the peace and security of a world without nuclear weapons," reiterating official U.S. policy—though more as a worthy, long-term goal best pursued incrementally than as an immediate objective. Obama also declared that the United States would remain nuclear-armed as long as other countries possessed stockpiles. According to statements he made in 2010, though, nuclear options would be a "last resort" and would not be available against non-nuclear states that were in compliance with nuclear nonproliferation norms.

Nuclear powers continue to make nuclear threats. Recently, Russian officials and Pakistan have said they would use their weapons if they deemed it necessary. At the same time, the United States appears to be entering a period of expanded nuclear budgets, in part because a critical mass of Pentagon planners still embrace outdated Cold War nuclear strategies, including that of first strike, in which the goal is to preemptively attack the opposing nation's arsenal in order to diminish or destroy its ability to retaliate. The Congressional Budget Office estimates that the United States is planning to spend $348 billionto maintain and modernize its nuclear arsenal over the next 10 years—an amount so great that it would establish (or strengthen) strong vested interests against abolition or even meaningful reduction. With prospects for U.S.

and Russian nuclear arms reductions at a standstill, the White House has not yet sought to rein in these exorbitant spending plans.

Citing nuclear competition with China and Russia, which are both modernizing their nuclear forces, the Pentagon justifies its budget goals with language and scenarios straight out of the Cold War. Joint Chiefs of Staff Vice Chairman James Winnefeld Jr. recently said to the House Armed Services Committee that Russian plans for mobile, land-based ICBMs worried him because they "would be hard for us to hit in a first strike." This statement is cause for concern because it shows that the Joint Chiefs of Staff believes there might come a time when the United States would want to launch a first strike.

Seventy years after the destruction of Hiroshima and Nagasaki, nuclear weapons remain in a special category, in which their use is narrowly circumscribed. They have become unusable except in the most unlikely circumstances, and their value as a deterrent lacks credibility because of the catastrophic dangers of mass and mutual destruction. U.S. presidents since Truman have come to realize that nuclear war is unwinnable.

Nonetheless, they have built up and to this day maintain forces that far exceed any calculation of what it requires to deter a nuclear attack. Today, the United States still has about 2,080 deployed nuclear warheads and Russia has some 1,780. Many of these weapons are primed for prompt launch and can reach their targets within 25 minutes. If these weapons were used even in a "limited" way, the result would be catastrophic nuclear devastation. This suggests that while the nuclear taboo still exists, the non-use legacy is at risk as long as defense officials in Russia and the United States continue to think and act in irresponsible Cold War terms, and the U.S. Senate refuses to ratify international restrictions on nuclear testing. As powerful a restraint as the taboo has been and may still be, complacency is foolhardy.

> *"While the nuclear taboo has helped to shift thinking on nuclear weapons, placing them outside of conventional warfare, ultimately it is not enough to ensure that these weapons will never be used."*

The Nuclear Taboo Is Not Enough

Eryn MacDonald

In this viewpoint, Eryn MacDonald argues that the nuclear taboo has played a role in preventing countries from using nuclear weapons since 1945. Countries realized that the use of nuclear weapons should be a last resort due to the horrific outcomes of an attack. However, in recent years Russian President Vladimir Putin has threatened the use of nuclear weapons in the country's conflict with Ukraine. According to MacDonald, nuclear threats threaten the nuclear taboo by raising doubts about its durability. As a result, the only way to eliminate the nuclear threat is by entirely eliminating nuclear weapons. Eryn MacDonald is an analyst with the Global Security Program of the Union of Concerned Scientists.

As you read, consider the following questions:

1. According to MacDonald, what relatively recent event has called into question the nuclear taboo?

"What Is the Nuclear Taboo and Is Putin About to Break It?" by Eryn MacDonald, Union of Concerned Scientists, March 16, 2022. Reprinted by permission. https://allthingsnuclear.org/emacdonald/what-is-the-nuclear-taboo-and-is-putin-about-to-break-it/.

2. According to Nina Tannenwald, what efforts were key in establishing the nuclear taboo?

3. How does the Treaty on the Prohibition of Nuclear Weapons (TPNW) differ from the Nuclear Nonproliferation Treaty (NPT)?

In 1945, the United States—at the time the world's only nuclear power—dropped two nuclear bombs on Hiroshima and Nagasaki, Japan. In the more than 75 years that followed, the United States and Soviet Union (USSR) engaged in a decades-long arms race, building tens of thousands of nuclear weapons and bringing the world to the brink of nuclear catastrophe thanks to multiple crises and repeated close calls due to human or computer error. Seven more states also developed nuclear weapons, but WWII remains the last time any state exploded a nuclear weapon in a conflict. This is even more notable since both the United States and the Soviet Union/Russia deployed shorter-range, lower-yield, tactical nuclear weapons and developed extensive plans—some of which still exist today—for their use in scenarios where they believed that they would be at a disadvantage in a conventional military conflict.

One explanation for this restraint is that countries developed a taboo against the use of nuclear weapons, coming to understand them as so horrific as to be essentially unusable except in the most extreme cases of last resort. But recent events—most notably Putin's attempt to use nuclear threats to hold the world hostage as he wages war on Ukraine—are calling into question the future of this taboo. After all, a taboo can always be broken. In the end the best way to ensure that the world is safe from nuclear weapons is to eliminate them completely.

What Is the "Nuclear Taboo"?

At the beginning of the atomic age, nuclear weapons, for all the devastation they caused in Japan, were expected to become just another weapon and to proliferate widely to any state that could develop them.

There was much debate among political and military leaders about their usefulness as a deterrent, but also on the battlefield. And although President Truman established nearly from the beginning that in the United States nuclear weapons should be legally under presidential control, physical control of these weapons remained in military hands. Early on, before safeguards were established, this meant that it might have been possible for military leaders to use them without a presidential order. President Eisenhower, among others, also gave military commanders the authority to use nuclear weapons in urgent situations when they could not reach the president (this is sometimes called pre-delegation of authority).

Over time, however, nuclear weapons became a category separate from other kinds of weapons, and refraining from using nuclear weapons became a new norm of international behavior, what scholar Nina Tannenwald termed the "nuclear taboo." Taboo here refers to "a particularly forceful kind of normative prohibition that is concerned with the protection of individuals and societies from behavior that is defined or perceived to be dangerous."

Tannenwald says this taboo is "associated with a widespread revulsion toward nuclear weapons and broadly held inhibitions on their use." She identifies the early and ongoing efforts of global grassroots antinuclear movements, nonnuclear weapon states, and nonstate actors like the United Nations—along with the eventual strategic nuclear stalemate between the U.S. and USSR—as key in establishing the nuclear taboo by stigmatizing and delegitimizing the use of nuclear weapons.

How Strong Is the Nuclear Taboo?

When states maintain a clear line between nuclear and conventional weapons, reserving nuclear weapons solely for deterrence of nuclear attacks, they help to strengthen the nuclear taboo. Ideally this would mean states declaring that they will never use nuclear weapons first, and backing this up with a nuclear doctrine and force posture that does not include nuclear warfighting capabilities. Out of all the nuclear powers, only China has consistently taken this step, but even its long-standing commitment to a minimal nuclear force may now be coming into question.

Unfortunately, in recent years the trend seems to be toward weakening, rather than strengthening, the nuclear taboo. Russia and the United States, along with some other nuclear armed states, have placed greater emphasis on tactical nuclear weapons—shorter-range and often lower-yield nuclear weapons designed to be used on the battlefield. These are particularly destabilizing since they can be perceived as more "usable" than the strategic weapons carried by intercontinental submarine-launched ballistic missiles. When nuclear weapons are seen as tools of warfighting—such as using tactical nuclear weapons to counter conventional military threats—the unique danger of nuclear weapons is blurred, and the taboo is weakened.

Nuclear threats, such as Putin's in Ukraine, also endanger the nuclear taboo. While they do not directly violate the taboo, they eat away at its foundation, raising doubts about its durability. Leaders who show a willingness to threaten nuclear use in any but the most dire of circumstances undermine the sense that nuclear weapons are so unthinkably abhorrent that their use should never be considered unless there is no question that the very existence of a state is in immediate danger.

The nuclear taboo is a norm, an unstated agreement on appropriate behavior that is strengthened by adherence over time but is not explicitly set out anywhere and is not in any way enforceable. A state that violates the taboo could face repercussions in the form of military action or economic sanctions. Or it could face social stigma that might have a less immediate impact, such as condemnation from other world leaders or censure at the United Nations. The consequences of breaking the nuclear taboo are, thankfully, so far unknown. But this means they are unknown not just to those who might break it, but also to those who must respond. Upholders of the taboo are left figuring out on the fly how to signal that such a violation will not go unpunished without further escalating a dangerous situation.

The Nuclear Taboo Is Not Enough

While the nuclear taboo has helped to shift thinking on nuclear weapons, placing them outside of conventional warfare, ultimately it is not enough to ensure that these weapons will never be used. As we are observing right now with Putin's loosely veiled threat that anyone interfering in his war on Ukraine will face "consequences they have never seen," some leaders will always try to push the boundaries, which can weaken or undermine the taboo. Whether or not such leaders ever truly intend to follow through with these threats, their words raise the level of tension in an already volatile situation, increasing the likelihood of a miscalculation or miscommunication that could lead to actual nuclear conflict.

It is encouraging, and perhaps some evidence for the durability of the nuclear taboo, that the United States and others have shown restraint in the face of Putin's threats, declining to raise their level of nuclear alert and, in the U.S. case, postponing a ballistic missile test that could have been seen as provocative. But one can easily imagine a situation in which this were not the reaction. In 2017, in response to North Korea's continued progress in its nuclear weapons program and Kim Jong Un's threats against the United States, President Trump issued his own nuclear threat. Such a reaction—as irresponsible as it was at the time—could have a much larger and more unpredictable impact in the current situation.

Eliminating Nuclear Threats Requires Eliminating Nuclear Weapons

The only way to put an end to nuclear threats, and the catastrophic potential that they will be carried out, is to eliminate the weapons themselves. This may seem utopian but it is actually a long-recognized goal.

The Nuclear Nonproliferation Treaty (NPT) recognized this almost 50 years ago, and most of the world—including nuclear powers—signed on. One of the objectives of the NPT is nuclear disarmament, but the treaty allowed, under what was supposed to be a temporary basis, the existence of a handful of recognized nuclear weapon states (the United States, Russia, China, France, and the United Kingdom). In the treaty, those nuclear weapon states committed themselves to negotiate an end to the nuclear arms race with the goal of complete nuclear disarmament, to be enshrined in "a treaty on general and complete disarmament under strict and effective international control." In exchange, the non-nuclear weapon states agreed not to pursue or acquire their own nuclear weapons.

The more recent Treaty on the Prohibition of Nuclear Weapons (TPNW) goes farther than the NPT, completely outlawing nuclear weapons on the way to eliminating them altogether. It aims to make the nuclear taboo international law. The TPNW has now been signed by 86 countries and ratified by 53; it entered into force on January 22, 2021. So far, none of the states that possess nuclear weapons have signed on. This is not surprising, since doing so would require them to commit to eliminating their nuclear arsenals by a specific date. But the treaty's recognition that nuclear use would have consequences for people living far beyond nuclear weapon states and its outright prohibition on such weapons with no exceptions for existing nuclear weapon states are an affirmation of much of the world's continuing commitment to maintaining the nuclear taboo.

Outside of treaties, some leaders, including U.S. and Russian presidents, have also explicitly called for the abolition of nuclear weapons. After their two countries spent decades building up their nuclear arsenals and facing repeated crises and close calls, President Reagan and Russian President Mikhail Gorbachev in 1986 nearly reached an agreement to eliminate all nuclear weapons by the year 2000. Negotiations ultimately broke down over disagreement on ballistic missile defenses, but both leaders had already stated their beliefs that elimination was possible, and desirable. Neither man was a utopian idealist, they had simply both seen first-hand the dangers of nuclear brinkmanship and understood that as long as nuclear weapons exist, so does the risk that they will be used.

First End the Current War, then Prevent the Next One

The war in Ukraine illustrates once again just how devastating even a conventional war is to the civilians who are caught up in its violence. The focus right now must be on preventing escalation, even if it does not reach the nuclear level, and ending Putin's violence against the Ukrainian people.

But in the long run, the war in Ukraine demonstrates once again how nuclear weapons—even when they remain unexploded in the background—complicate conflicts. They raise the risk of escalation, intentional or mistaken, to an unimaginable level. Perhaps this most recent reminder can help serve as a catalyst to finally move towards the only real solution to the nuclear weapons problem—elimination.

> *"Given the strained relations between countries, it may seem that the world is sitting on a ticking time bomb. However, despite this, the logic of nuclear deterrence brings reassurance."*

Nuclear Deterrence Is Still at Work Today

Meher Manga

While some argue that nuclear deterrence is an outdated concept and no longer applicable in a post-Cold War world, in this viewpoint Meher Manga argues that nuclear deterrence still plays a major role in preventing nuclear war today. Nuclear deterrence operates on the logic that countries are deterred from launching a nuclear attack on one another because they know the other country will also retaliate with a nuclear attack. World leaders today are still aware of the devastation that a nuclear attack could cause, and countries continue to maintain nuclear arsenals under the assumption that nuclear deterrence still works. At the time this viewpoint was published, Meher Manga was an intern with the Observer Research Foundation.

As you read, consider the following questions:

1. What are some of the arguments against the logic of nuclear deterrence mentioned in this viewpoint?

"The Relevance of Nuclear Deterrence in a Post-Cold War World," by Meher Manga, Observer Research Foundation, July 12, 2021. Reprinted by permission.

2. Where is the logic of nuclear deterrence playing out today, according to this viewpoint?

3. According to Manga, in what nuclear scenario would the logic of nuclear deterrence likely fail?

At the brink of the Cuban Missile Crisis of 1962, the world narrowly escaped what could have been a nuclear war between the erstwhile Soviet Union (USSR) and the United States (U.S.). Since then, many countries have built up their nuclear arsenals, especially the ones that are at loggerheads with each other, the most obvious ones being Pakistan and India. However, the pertinent question is: Despite officially nine countries having nuclear weapons, why has the world been able to avoid a nuclear war? The answer to this question provided by International Relations theorists is the "logic of nuclear deterrence," which was propagated by academics such as Thomas Schelling and BD Berkowitz during the Cold War. However, is this logic still relevant to explain nuclear conflicts in a post-Cold War world order?

It is undisputed that the world scenario has changed since the collapse of the Soviet Union and the end of bipolarity. As the struggle for power between China and the U.S. intensifies, there is a growing concern about the nuclear weapons that China has and its potential to use those weapons against the U.S. and its regional rival India. Then, there is North Korea that has continuously declined Washington DC's proposal for denuclearisation and continues to build nuclear weapons. This article argues that despite these rivalries, the world has been able to avoid a nuclear war and the logic of nuclear deterrence should be given some credit for this.

Understanding the Logic of Nuclear Deterrence

The basic principle of this logic is: One actor prevents another from taking some action by raising the latter's fear of the consequences that will ensue. Hypothetically, if Country A launches a nuclear war against Country B, Country B will be able to inflict enough damage on Country A that it would lead to what theorists call "mutually assured destruction." Thus, in a nuclear war, both sides will be so badly harmed that it will be impossible to declare one side or the other as the winner. Even if one of them tries to attack and disable the nuclear weapons of its rival, the other would still be left with enough nuclear weapons to inflict unacceptable destruction.

Kenneth Waltz has explained the logic behind nuclear deterrence in a simple yet profound manner: "Although we are defenceless, if you attack we will punish you to an extent that more than cancels your gains." Thus, it helps avoid a nuclear war as each side tries to secure their interests by avoiding a nuclear confrontation.

The Logic of Nuclear Deterrence in a Bipolar World

Even though the USSR had a nuclear stockpile of 40,000 nuclear weapons and the U.S. had a nuclear stockpile of 30,000 nuclear weapons, they did not engage in a nuclear war. An analysis of the Cuban Missile Crisis illustrates that at its peak, a nuclear war between the superpowers almost seemed inevitable. However, the leaders were firm about not engaging in a nuclear war as it would cause destruction to both the superpowers. This is what prompted the U.S. to intercept Soviet warships rather than engage directly and Moscow to passively withdraw. Deterrence led to negotiation between the superpowers as the Soviet Union agreed to remove the missiles from Cuba, while the U.S. promised not to invade Cuba and President Kennedy even agreed to remove American missiles from Turkey.

Problems with the Logic of Nuclear Deterrence

Nevertheless, there are many scholars who have expressed their scepticism about the logic of deterrence by arguing that just because it avoided a nuclear confrontation between the Soviet Union and the U.S., it does not mean it is a "proven fact." Nuclear strategists have urged leaders to exercise caution when basing their security strategies on this logic. For instance, North Korea threatening to wage a nuclear war against the U.S. has raised doubts in the minds of many advisors and academics.

Then there is the question of the credibility of this line of thinking: Should countries base their security strategies on a logic? Many have argued that the logic of nuclear deterrence is not an established norm but a "hypothesis" and, thus, basing a nation's security strategy on it is a gamble. Nuclear deterrence is based on the assumption that a country will avoid starting a nuclear war in order to protect its own security.

Another major flaw with this logic is the presence of many uncontrollable variables such as the misuse of nuclear weapons if the control falls into the hands of the wrong people or a soldier deliberately starting a nuclear war to create mischief.

Why the Logic of Nuclear Deterrence Is Not Redundant in a Post-Cold War Society

Given the strained relations between countries, it may seem that the world is sitting on a ticking time bomb. However, despite this, the logic of nuclear deterrence brings reassurance. First, there is the cost-benefit analysis of a nuclear war. It is a given that nuclear weapons can bring so much destruction that the costs of war will outweigh the benefits and this would "deter" leaders from engaging in nuclear warfare. There is a renewed threat of "second-strike capability" that keeps countries from engaging in nuclear warfare.

Second, leaders who are driven by personal interests are aware of the fact that no winner would emerge from a nuclear war. Given the nuclear threats by Kim Jong-un to the U.S., it may seem that there is a possibility of North Korean nuclear attacks. However, why has Pyongyang not acted on these threats? The main reason is that Kim Jong-un understands that waging a nuclear war would result in "mutual destruction" and this has restrained him from a nuclear attack.

Another good illustration of this logic at play is South Asia — a volatile region with three nuclear powers who are at loggerheads with each other. Despite China, India, and Pakistan having nuclear weapons, the region has been able to avoid a nuclear confrontation. Pakistan and India became nuclear states in 1998 and have fought one war since then. However, the Kargil War fought in 1999 did not see the use of any nuclear weapons. The Deputy Foreign Minister of Pakistan at the time, Shamshad Ahmed, told a Pakistani newspaper that Pakistan is willing to use "any weapon in our arsenal to defend our territorial integrity." To this, George Fernandez, India's then Defence Minister, responded that in doing so they would "liquidate" their own country in the process. This shows how nuclear deterrence plays out when indirect threats are made from either side. On analysing Sino-Indian relations, particularly the Ladakh stand-off of 2020, it is evident that both countries are careful to not use nuclear weapons even as a threat. Both these countries have stated that the role of the weapon is narrowly framed for safeguarding against nuclear blackmail and coercion. Both have declared No First Use (NFU) positions.

Thus, nuclear deterrence is not just a Cold War term but is extremely valid in a post-Cold War scenario. Countries have understood the importance of nuclear deterrence and it plays an important role in designing their security strategies. It is used by countries as a bargaining chip to deter nuclear retaliation by other countries. However, it should be noted that nuclear deterrence is not the only answer to security problems and its application can be enhanced by using other strategies such as peace talks and confidence-building measures. While it is evident that countries have understood the importance of nuclear deterrence, the world faces the threat of nuclear attack by non-state actors as deterrence as a strategy may likely fail in such cases.

"Perhaps the 'MAD' acronym of the phenomenon is a good fit when we consider that all of this money is being wasted on weapons that are hopefully never to be used. Would it not make more sense to not have these weapons at all?"

Mutually Assured Destruction Causes Mutually Assured Distrust

The Decision Lab

In this viewpoint from the Decision Lab, the author explains that despite the fact that mutually assured destruction is often considered a key concept in the strategy to prevent nuclear war, it is also what causes countries to grow and maintain their nuclear arsenals. The USSR engaged in the arms race with the U.S. after the U.S. bombed Hiroshima and Nagasaki because they did not want to suffer the same sort of attack, and having nuclear weapons to use in a counterattack seemed like the best way to prevent this. Mutually assured destruction is fundamentally based on mutual distrust, since no country trusts that its adversaries would not attack them. Mutually assured destruction is an expensive strategy and a dangerous one, since there have been numerous close calls for intentional and accidental nuclear attacks. The Decision Lab is an applied research and innovation firm.

"Mutually Assured Destruction," The Decision Lab. Reprinted by permission. https://thedecisionlab.com/reference-guide/management/mutually-assured-destruction.

As you read, consider the following questions:

1. What is equilibrium theory, according to this viewpoint?
2. Who coined the term "mutually assured destruction"?
3. What are some examples of mutually assured destruction from everyday life mentioned in this viewpoint?

If mutually assured destruction sounds like a daunting concept, that's because it is. It is a military strategy used in wars or combat where if either side makes an attack, the destruction of both sides is ensured. As a result, in this situation, a stalemate arises. Peace is ensured through a guarantee that each side has the ability to destroy the other and will do so if necessary.

Although mainly a term used in military strategy and jargon, the foundations of mutually assured destruction, competition, and trust are also relevant to aspects of our relationships with others today.[1]

We often find ourselves in competitive environments, especially when it comes to the workplace. While our desire to "win," or succeed, is often at the forefront of our justification for making particular decisions, the mutually assured destruction phenomenon asks us to what end and at what cost we are willing to participate in those behaviors. If we behave in a particular way to advance our own careers—such as exposing a coworker for dropping the ball on a project, for example—we are likely to meet retaliation—that coworker might respond by informing the boss, for instance. A level of trust must therefore be maintained between us and our competitors, to avoid a snowball of everyone's suffering.

Knowing that we are in a relationship in which mutual destruction is at risk therefore begs the question: Is it worth it to make a move?

I gain nothing by having a rock in my boxing glove if the other fellow has one too.

– A quote from Sax Rohmer's book The Shadow of Fu-Manchu[2]

Key Terms

- Nuclear Deterrence: A military strategy that uses the threat of retaliation to dissuade a nation from a particular kind of attack. When it comes to nuclear bombs, deterrence is achieved by the promise of a nation responding to a nuclear bomb attack with their own nuclear bomb attack.[3]
- Bomber Gap: During the race to make the best hydrogen bomb, President Dwight D. Eisenhower believed that the Soviet Union had more bomber planes—the preferred vehicle for dropping bombs at this time—causing him to believe there was a "bomber gap" and order more planes to be made.[4] This kind of behavior shows that due to mutually assured destruction, nations feel the need to constantly keep up with other nations' technological developments so that everyone has an "equal" opportunity to retaliate.
- Equilibrium Strategy: A theory developed by John von Neumann, which suggests that if all players in a situation maintain the same strategy, it is best for you to maintain this same strategy as well.[5] It plays into mutually assured destruction as it suggests that the best course of action for nations is to do nothing, as long as other nations stick to doing nothing as well.

History

On August 6th, 1945, an American pilot dropped the first ever deployed atomic bomb over Hiroshima, Japan, immediately killing 80,000 people. Three days later, another atomic bomb was released over the Japanese city of Nagasaki, killing another 40,000 people.[6] Essentially, these events ended World War II—but at what cost?

After the deployment of the first atomic bomb came a race between other nations to develop this same cruel weaponry. The Soviet Union did not want to find themselves in the same position as Japan in the event that they engaged in a war with the U.S. They began to work towards creating hydrogen bombs that would have an even more devastating impact than atomic bombs. The U.S. responded by equally dedicating time, effort and resources into developing their own hydrogen bomb. Not before long, other nations got in on the action.[4]

Somewhere within the nuclear arms race, nations seemed to forget one fundamental truth: we are all human and we are all in this together. If one country dropped a nuclear bomb, others would retaliate, and before long, all of humanity would perish.[1] This is where nuclear deterrence was developed—since both the Soviet Union and the U.S. had nuclear bombs, they dissuaded one another from using them with the threat of retaliation. One nuclear bomb would become a catalyst for dozens more and no nation would emerge victorious—in other words, a lose-lose situation.[4]

This is where mutually assured destruction comes in. Since multiple nations have nuclear bombs they could deploy, any one country deploying them would result in the destruction of nations and a majority of humanity. Knowing that worldwide, humanity would suffer from the deployment of a nuclear bomb forces each nation with nuclear bombs into a stalemate. The fear of retaliation inhibits action. Reverting to the childlike tendency of "I won't if you won't," the development of mutually assured destruction as a result of nuclear bombs is actually a method of peacekeeping. It is a rational response to the knowledge that acting would lead to one's own destruction.

The term mutually assured destruction, often referred to by its acronym "MAD," was coined by physicist and game theorist John von Neumann, who was an important figure in the development of U.S. nuclear devices.[7] Based on his equilibrium strategy, nations realized that the best attack to avoid mutually assured destruction was no attack at all.

Consequences

Although mutually assured destruction is likely only a term familiar to military strategists, the phenomenon has important implications for regular people's lives. Most simply, it helps keep us alive. Unfortunately, nations don't seem to trust one another enough to live peacefully without the threat of weapons, which makes mutually assured destruction necessary. It is a unique brand of trust based on knowing the other nation will not do anything because they too will suffer in the end. When disagreements occur between political leaders, nuclear deterrence means that hopefully, no nation will choose to unleash the devastation weapon.

WHY MUTUALLY ASSURED DESTRUCTION DOESN'T WORK

Nuclear deterrence doesn't work. Here's why.

1. We aren't rational and we can't read minds. For nuclear deterrence to work, all stakeholders must be perceived to act "rationally" and "predictably" but we know that's not how people work—particularly in the fog of war.
2. Nuclear weapons don't keep the peace. History shows that the existence of nuclear weapons has done nothing to prevent the many terrible conflicts since 1945, including acts of aggression against countries with nuclear weapons. In reality, nuclear weapons haven't been used due solely to good luck—which cannot be expected to last forever.
3. Nuclear weapons make conflicts worse. The 2022 Russian invasion of Ukraine highlights how any of the 9 nuclear-armed states can threaten or use nuclear weapons to limit the capacity of other states to respond.
4. Nuclear deterrence makes nuclear use more likely because the threat of use of nuclear weapons must be credible, and so the nuclear armed states are always poised to launch nuclear weapons.
5. Nuclear weapons are useless for today's threats. Nuclear weapons are strategically useless to address the actual security threats facing nations in the 21st century, including climate change, terrorism and cyber attacks.

"What About 'Nuclear Deterrence' Theory? Do Nuclear Weapons Help Keep the Peace?" ICAN.

Outside of military strategy, the fundamental principles behind mutually assured destruction might play into other areas of our lives. The idea is based on a sense of competition between two parties and the knowledge that the opposition has the ability to retaliate. Mutually assured destruction therefore promotes good behavior between both parties in any situation—friendship, professionalism, or politics—because rationally, no one wants to suffer themselves. It essentially draws on the lesson, "treat others how you want to be treated," as it seems common sense to understand that you will get back the same behavior you dole out. The idea might therefore incentivize coworkers to have each other's backs or inspire friends to keep each other's secrets, expecting the same courtesies in return.

However, mutually assured destruction might also enable bad behavior. Two businesses might engage in tax fraud together, which provides assurance that neither business will tell the authorities because both are implicated in the fraud.[1] Law enforcement sometimes draws on its understanding of this practice by offering lighter punishments to those who rat out their accomplices.

Controversies

Mutually assured destruction is based on the principle that if a particular weapon is used in an attack, the nation being attacked will be able to retaliate with equal force and destruction. What this means is that countries pour millions of dollars into the development of new-and-improved technology only to keep up with one another, similarly to Eisenhower's response to the perceived bomber gap in the 1950s. Perhaps the "MAD" acronym of the phenomenon is a good fit when we consider that all of this money is being wasted on weapons that are hopefully never to be used. Would it not make more sense to not have these weapons at all?

However, there is some evidence that mutually assured destruction doesn't actually work. Although no nuclear war has killed off humanity to this day, there have been a lot of close calls. The Cuban Missile Crisis brought us close to a nuclear holocaust.

After the U.S. found out that the Soviet Union installed nuclear-armed missiles in Cuba, close to U.S. soil, the U.S. claimed it was ready to use military force to neutralize this threat if necessary.[9] If the U.S. had acted, we might not be here today.

Lastly, even if it does work, a deterrence strategy might not be a long-term sustainable solution, since it is actually based on a lack of trust. Instead of trusting that peace will be kept between nations, countries feel the need to develop weaponry they can leverage should the need arise. This makes the strategy prone to escalating tensions, accidents, or extremist governments that lack concern for the overall good of humanity.[9] If one nation develops an even more powerful weapon, will the rest of the world insist on keeping up? Where will we draw the line?

The Prisoner's Dilemma

The prisoner's dilemma is a classic philosophical thought experiment that shows why acting in one's own self-interest often results in worse consequences than working together with others. It provides evidence that mutually assured destruction should be considered when making decisions, as it can benefit both competing parties.

The classic prisoner's dilemma narrative is about two individuals who have been arrested and are being interrogated about a bank robbery. The authorities have only these two individuals as witnesses and will only be able to prove a case if one of them betrays the other and testifies as an accomplice. If both remain silent, the authorities will only be able to convict each of them on a charge of loitering (one year in jail each). If only one testifies, and the other stays silent, the one who testifies will go free while the other one will receive a three-year jail sentence. If both testify, each will receive a two-year sentence.[10]

In this scenario, it may seem like the rational choice is to testify because assuming your accomplice does not testify, this choice leaves you with the least amount of jail time. Plus, if you do not testify, you risk unfairly going to jail for much longer than your accomplice. If each individual does testify, however, they will end up with two years' jail time each (more than the minimum). However, in an ideal scenario, if both criminals here realize that there is mutually assured destruction, they will both do nothing, resulting in only one year of jail time each. The dilemma provides evidence for the equilibrium strategy, as the best move is no move— but it is dependent on a high degree of trust between both parties that the other side will cooperate.

When MAD Doesn't Work: Mutually Assured Distrust

Mutually assured destruction only achieves peace when the bearers of the arms have an equal amount of power. A nation will only stop themselves from attacking another nation if they believe the attack will result in their own destruction as well. If there is a power imbalance, such deterrence is not likely.

One modern-day example of the power imbalance disabling the peace of mutually assured destruction is the historical relationship between Black people and police officers. Unfortunately, implicit biases often make police subconsciously fearful of people of color, due to stereotypes that people of color are dangerous. This implicit bias leads police to act in particularly hostile ways towards people of color, particularly Black men. Yet, this biased fear does not prevent police officers from acting—they do not believe that there will be "mutually assured destruction," despite their belief that Black people are dangerous—because they have the law (and guns) on their side. The uneven potential for destruction all too often leads to unwarranted killings of Black people, with police afterward claiming they "feared for their life."

The mutually assured distrust can cause minority communities to retaliate, which then causes law enforcement to (often violently) crack down on riots and retaliations.[11] The cycle appears similar to one where mutually assured destruction would prevent further attack, however, because police officers hold more power, they are not afraid of making the first attack. In order for mutually assured destruction to work, police officers must learn not to abuse their authority. Alternatively, a different tactic that aims at improving the trust and relationship between police officers and racialized individuals needs to be employed.

Sources

1. Farnam Street. (2020, November 28). *Mutually Assured Destruction: When Not to Play.* https://fs.blog/2017/06/mutually-assured-destruction/
2. Goodreads. (n.d.). *Mutually Assured Destruction Quotes.* Retrieved February 27, 2021, from https://www.goodreads.com/quotes/tag/mutually-assured-destruction
3. Encyclopedia Britannica. (2017, June 12). *Deterrence.* https://www.britannica.com/topic/deterrence-political-and-military-strategy
4. Encyclopedia Britannica. (2020, July 17). *Mutual assured destruction.* https://www.britannica.com/topic/mutual-assured-destruction
5. Chen, J. (2020, February 3). *Nash Equilibrium.* Investopedia. https://www.investopedia.com/terms/n/nash-equilibrium.asp
6. History. (2009, November 18). *Bombing of Hiroshima and Nagasaki.* https://www.history.com/topics/world-war-ii/bombing-of-hiroshima-and-nagasaki
7. Wilde, R. (2020, June 20). *What Is Mutually Assured Destruction?* ThoughtCo. https://www.thoughtco.com/mutually-assured-destruction-1221190
8. History. (2010, January 4). *Cuban Missile Crisis.* https://www.history.com/topics/cold-war/cuban-missile-crisis
9. Shermer, M. (2014, June 1). *Will Mutual Assured Destruction Continue to Deter Nuclear War?* Scientific American. https://www.scientificamerican.com/article/will-mutual-assured-destruction-continue-to-deter-nuclear-war/
10. Investopedia. (2021, January 1). *Prisoner's Dilemma.* https://www.investopedia.com/terms/p/prisoners-dilemma.asp
11. Observer. (2016, June 12). *Mutually Assured Distrust.* https://observer.com/2016/07/mutually-assured-distrust/

Periodical and Internet Sources Bibliography

The following articles have been selected to supplement the diverse views presented in this chapter.

"Strengthening the Nuclear Taboo in the Midst of Russia's War on Ukraine," Arms Control Association, February 22, 2023. https://www.armscontrol.org/issue-briefs/2023-02/strengthening-nuclear-taboo-midst-russias-war-ukraine.

Seth Baum, "How to Evaluate the Risk of Nuclear War," BBC, March 10, 2022. https://www.bbc.com/future/article/20220309-how-to-evaluate-the-risk-of-nuclear-war.

Yuriy Gorodnichenko and Torbjörn Becker, "NATO Must Get MAD at Russia," Project Syndicate, March 17, 2022. https://www.project-syndicate.org/commentary/nato-russia-nuclear-threat-mutual-assured-destruction-by-yuriy-gorodnichenko-and-torbjorn-becker-2022-03.

Amy J. Nelson and Alexander H. Montgomery, "How Not to Estimate the Likelihood of Nuclear War," Brookings Institution, October 19, 2022. https://www.brookings.edu/blog/order-from-chaos/2022/10/19/how-not-to-estimate-the-likelihood-of-nuclear-war/.

Tanya Ogilvie-White, "As Putin Puts Nuclear Forces on High Alert, Here Are 5 Genuine Nuclear Dangers for Us All," Conversation, February 27, 2022. https://theconversation.com/as-putin-puts-nuclear-forces-on-high-alert-here-are-5-genuine-nuclear-dangers-for-us-all-177923.

Barry Pavel and Christian Trotti, "New Tech Will Erode Nuclear Deterrence. The U.S. Must Adapt," Defense One, November 4, 2021. https://www.defenseone.com/ideas/2021/11/new-tech-will-erode-nuclear-deterrence-us-must-adapt/186634/.

Commander Daniel Post, "The Value and Limits of Nuclear Deterrence," U.S. Naval Institute, January 2023. https://www.usni.org/magazines/proceedings/2023/january/value-and-limits-nuclear-deterrence.

Matthew Rozsa, "Experts Once Thought Mutually Assured Destruction Would Prevent Nuclear War. Now They're Not So

Sure," Salon, March 11, 2022. https://www.salon.com/2022/03/11/mutually-assured-destruction-psychology/.

Paul D. Shinkman, "Putin's Hollow Nuclear Threat," *U.S. News & World Report*, February 24, 2023. https://www.usnews.com/news/the-report/articles/2023-02-24/why-ukraine-wont-lead-putin-to-nuclear-war.

Nina Tannenwald, "The Vanishing Nuclear Taboo?" *Foreign Affairs*, October 15, 2018. https://www.foreignaffairs.com/articles/world/2018-10-15/vanishing-nuclear-taboo.

For Further Discussion

Chapter 1

1. According to the viewpoints in this chapter, how has the nuclear geopolitical situation changed since the Cold War?
2. Based on what you've read in the viewpoints in this chapter, what are some of the challenges faced today in nuclear arms control?
3. According to the viewpoint by Deborah Netburn, nuclear anxiety has faded since the Cold War because other bigger existential threats have emerged, such as terrorism and climate change. Do you think nuclear warfare is reemerging as a major existential threat? Use evidence from the viewpoints to support your answer.

Chapter 2

1. Based on what you read in the viewpoints in this chapter, do you think the U.S. should possess nuclear weapons? Explain your answer.
2. According to the viewpoint from NATO, one of its primary goals is nuclear disarmament, but it also insists that it considers maintaining a nuclear arsenal essential as long as other countries have them. Do you think this is contradictory? Why or why not?
3. According to the viewpoint from Zachary Keck, what is brinkmanship in relation to nuclear strategy? Does this seem like an effective strategy? Why or why not?

Chapter 3

1. According to the viewpoints in this chapter, what are some of the main obstacles to forming nuclear agreements between countries?

2. What are some of the suggestions presented in this chapter for how to encourage countries to form nuclear agreements?

3. As the viewpoints in this chapter suggest, some nuclear treaties are focused on nuclear nonproliferation (preventing countries from developing or acquiring more nuclear weapons), while others are focused on nuclear disarmament (making it so that no country possesses any nuclear weapons). Which type of agreement do you think seems most effective? Explain your answer.

Chapter 4

1. Based on the viewpoints you read in this chapter, does the nuclear taboo or mutually assured destruction seem more effective at nuclear deterrence? Explain your reasoning.

2. According to the viewpoints in this chapter, what are some of the challenges to the doctrines of mutually assured destruction and the nuclear taboo faced today?

3. According to the viewpoint by Eryn MacDonald, Russian President Vladimir Putin's threats to use nuclear weapons in Russia's war with Ukraine erodes the nuclear taboo. Do you agree with this argument? Why or why not?

Organizations to Contact

The editors have compiled the following list of organizations concerned with the issues debated in this book. The descriptions are derived from materials provided by the organizations. All have publications or information available for interested readers. The list was compiled on the date of publication of the present volume; the information provided here may change. Be aware that many organizations take several weeks or longer to respond to inquiries, so allow as much time as possible.

Arms Control Association

1200 18th Street NW, Suite 1175
Washington, DC 20036
(202) 463-8270
website: www.armscontrol.org

The Arms Control Association is a U.S. national nonpartisan membership organization that is dedicated to promoting public understanding of and support for effective arms control policies. They use public education and media programs to help policymakers, the press, and the public better understand the issues related to arms control.

Atomic Heritage Foundation

601 Eubank Blvd SE
Albuquerque, NM 87123
(505) 245-2137
website: https://ahf.nuclearmuseum.org

The Atomic Heritage Foundation is dedicated to preserving the history of the Manhattan Project through preserving the accounts of people who participated in it and by supporting the Manhattan Project National Historical Park. It is a project of the National Museum of Nuclear History, which is intended to educate the public about the Atomic Age, from early nuclear development to peaceful applications of nuclear technology today.

Bulletin of the Atomic Scientists

1307 East 60th Street
Chicago, IL 60637
(773) 702-6308
email: admin@thebulletin.org
website: https://thebulletin.org

The Bulletin of the Atomic Scientists is an independent nonprofit organization dedicated to publishing information tracking man-made threats such as nuclear weapons. The organization began in 1945 after the atomic bombings of Hiroshima and Nagasaki and has continued ever since. It publishes free-access articles on its website and a bi-monthly nontechnical academic journal on science and global security issues, and it is responsible for the Doomsday Clock, which symbolizes the likelihood of human-made global catastrophe.

International Atomic Energy Association (IAEA)

Vienna International Centre
PO Box 100
1400 Vienna, Austria
(+43-1) 2600-0
email: iaeany@un.org
website: www.iaea.org

The International Atomic Energy Association (IAEA) is an intergovernmental forum for safe, secure, and peaceful uses of nuclear science and technology. It maintains and supports programs that encourage the use of nuclear energy and emphasizes nuclear safety.

International Campaign to Abolish Nuclear Weapons (ICAN)

Place de Cornavin 2
1201 Geneva, Switzerland
+41 22 788 20 63
email: info@icanw.org
website: www.icanw.org

The International Campaign to Abolish Nuclear Weapons (ICAN) is a coalition of nongovernmental organizations from 100 countries that promotes adherence to and implementation of the United Nations Treaty on the Prohibition of Nuclear Weapons. It is focused on mobilizing civil society around the world to prohibit and eliminate nuclear weapons.

National Nuclear Security Administration (NNSA)

1000 Independence Ave., SW
Washington, DC 20585
(202) 586-5000
website: www.energy.gov/nnsa/national-nuclear-security-administration

The National Nuclear Security Administration (NNSA) is a semi-autonomous U.S. federal agency that is responsible for ensuring national security through the military application of nuclear science. Its parent agency is the Department of Energy, and its mission is to manage the U.S. nuclear weapons stockpile, to reduce the global danger of nuclear weapons through promoting nonproliferation and safe nuclear practices, and to provide the U.S. Navy with safe and effective nuclear propulsion plants.

Nuclear Threat Initiative (NTI)

1776 Eye Street, NW
Suite 600
Washington, DC 20006
(202) 296-4810
email: contact@nti.org
website: www.nti.org

The Nuclear Threat Initiative (NTI) is a nonprofit, nonpartisan global security organization focused on reducing nuclear threats. NTI has four policy programs: the Global Nuclear Policy Program, Nuclear Materials Security, Scientific and Technical Affairs, and Global Biological Policy and Programs.

Union of Concerned Scientists

Two Brattle Square
Cambridge, MA 02138
(617) 547-5552
website: www.ucsusa.org

The Union of Concerned Scientists is a nonprofit science advocacy organization based in the U.S. whose members include private citizens and professional scientists. Its mission is to use rigorous science to solve the planet's most pressing problems, including addressing the threats posed by nuclear weapons.

United Nations Office for Disarmament Affairs (UNODA)

Information and Outreach Branch
UN Plaza
Room S-3024
New York, NY 10017
email: UNODA-web@un.org
website: www.un.org/disarmament

The United Nations Office for Disarmament Affairs (UNODA) is an office of the UN Secretariat that promotes nuclear disarmament and nonproliferation across the globe. It supports regional disarmament efforts and preventative measures.

U.S. Department of Defense (DOD)

1400 Defense Pentagon
Washington, DC 20301
(202) 461-7600
website: www.defense.gov

The U.S. Department of Defense is an executive branch department of the federal government that is responsible for coordinating and supervising all agencies and functions related to the armed forces and national security. It is the largest branch of the U.S. government and is responsible for deterring war and ensuring national security.

Bibliography of Books

Rizwana Abbasi. *Building a Road to Nuclear Disarmament* (Innovations in International Affairs). London, UK: Routledge, 2022.

David A. Cooper. *Arms Control for the Third Nuclear Age: Between Disarmament and Armageddon.* Washington, DC: Georgetown University Press, 2023.

Stephen P. Friot. *Containing History: How Cold War History Explains US-Russia Relations.* Norman, OK: University of Oklahoma Press, 2023.

Rose Gottemoeller. *Negotiating the New START Treaty* (Rapid Communications in Conflict and Security). Amherst, NY: Cambria Press, 2021.

Yogesh Joshi and Frank O'Donnell. *India and Nuclear Asia: Forces, Doctrine, and Dangers.* Washington, DC: Georgetown University Press, 2018.

Haq Kamar, ed. *Nuclear Anxiety* (At Issue). New York, NY: Greenhaven Publishing, 2020.

Edward Kaplan. *To Kill Nations: American Strategy in the Air-Atomic Age and the Rise of Mutually Assured Destruction.* Ithaca, NY: Cornell University Press, 2020.

Samuel S. Kloda. *The Atomic Bomb in Images and Documents: The Manhattan Project and the Bombing of Hiroshima and Nagasaki.* Jefferson, NC: McFarland, 2023.

Michael Krepon. *Winning and Losing the Nuclear Peace: The Rise, Demise, and Revival of Arms Control.* Stanford, CA: Stanford University Press, 2021.

Matthew Kroenig. *The Logic of American Nuclear Strategy: Why Strategic Superiority Matters* (Bridging the Gap). New York, NY: Oxford University Press, 2020.

James H. Lebovic. *The False Promise of Superiority: The United States and Nuclear Deterrence After the Cold War.* New York, NY: Oxford University Press, 2023.

Vipin Narang and Scott D. Sagan, eds. *The Fragile Balance of Terror: Deterrence in the New Nuclear Age* (Cornell Studies in Security Affairs). Ithaca, NY: Cornell University Press, 2023.

David Patrikarakos. *Nuclear Iran: The Birth of an Atomic State.* Paperback ed. London, UK: I.B. Tauris, 2021.

Ramesh Thakur, ed. *The Nuclear Ban Treaty: A Transformational Reframing of the Global Nuclear Order.* London, UK: Routledge, 2021.

Aiden Warren and Joseph M. Siracusa. *US Presidents and Cold War Nuclear Diplomacy* (The Evolving American Presidency). London, UK: Palgrave Macmillan, 2021.

Index

3190106955001